SMASHING
SERENDIPITY

This is dedicated to my husband Percy, my children James, Aaron, Alice and Shannon Kearing and their partners, my grandchildren and great-grandchildren. Thank you for the love and support you have given me, and for your patience and interest in the many stories I have told over the years. Also to Mum and Dad and the old spirits who, by the grace of God, have protected and guided me throughout my life.

This story is inspired by actual events. I have changed the names of the people out of respect for them and others who are now deceased. The Nyoongar words used in the story are Binjarib specific, as taught to me by my mother.

SMASHING SERENDIPITY

THE STORY OF ONE MOORDITJ YORGA

LOUISE K. HANSEN

 FREMANTLE PRESS

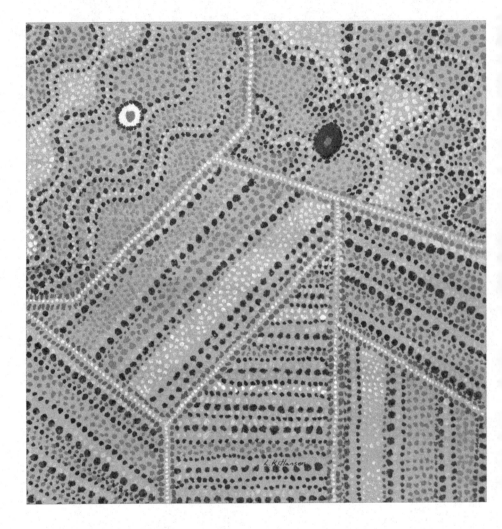

'Two Worlds', 2014
by Louise K. Hansen (12.5.1950–24.7.2022)
60 × 60 cm, acrylic on canvas

This painting tells the story of my parents' respective birth countries. The top orange half depicts Dad's Palyku land in the Pilbara in its original state before mining. It has all natural vegetation and food sources, uncleared with fresh water and rivers running through it. It is a beautiful but harsh land.

The bottom half shows Mum's Nyoongar country and how, since colonisation, it has been cleared of nearly all its virgin bushland. It is fenced off. It too is quite beautiful but our people can no longer access areas that used to contain our songlines and stories, or any that may have had significance to us. We cannot hunt there anymore. It is now used for farming, with rows and rows of planted crops and trees. The land is very green, organised and structured to accommodate eventual harvesting.

In the top half of the painting there are two circles, one dark brown with a red centre and one white with a red centre. The dark brown one represents my Dad's mother – my grandmother. The white one represents my Irish grandfather. They fell in love. And their skin may have been different but they had at least one thing in common. Both had red blood.

CONTENTS

KARLA WAANGKINY

It was a balmy summer evening and my son had just stoked the big fire. Even though we were camped nearly a hundred yards away from the river, there was a chilly wind coming directly off the water. I had rugged up with a warm jacket and an old blanket and sat alongside my grandchildren taking in the warmth and marvelling at the patterns created by the sparks that flew into the darkening sky. More sparks flew as my son put even more wood on the fire. The flare-up from the flames made it seem like the Milky Way was within arm's reach.

Except for two boys and a young girl, all my grandchildren were adults, some with children of their own, and those little great-grannies were now sound asleep. It was early summer and Biruk was upon us, so as a family we had travelled down to the Bend, some three miles west of Pinjarra, to camp a few nights and do a bit of fishing.

'So, you young ones looking for a good story about our mob, are you?' I asked.

'Yeah Nan, tell us some ghost stories,' said one of the little ones.

'Well, I'll leave the ghost stories for later, when it gets a bit darker. They will sound so much scarier then. What would you like to know?'

My grandson Bruce said, 'Nan, tell us about your life. You hardly ever let us know what it was like back in the days when you were young.'

I pondered the question for a while, watching the dancing flames. There was so much I could say. To gather my thoughts and to give myself time to consider what to tell them I said, 'On one condition, Bruce. First, you get me a cup of tea and a piece of that dampa your mum made. Make sure to put some quandong jam on it, please.'

After a couple of sips of tea, I began.

'So you want to know about me and my life? Okay, I will tell you part of it. It's about me and my Nyoongar family and our lives in Pinjarra. You gotta realise though, what I tell you is coming from my own experience. It's what I have lived through myself and what I have been told by our old people. Like it or not, it deserves to be respected.

'The main purpose for me telling you now is for your information. You lot. My children, grandchildren and great-grandchildren. I reckon you all need to know about the past. At least some of the things that I have experienced in my lifetime. Also what my Elders, your ancestors, have been through. It is only some of what our Nyoongar families have had to endure, just to survive.'

For a few moments there was total silence. Then I started to talk, and apart from my voice, the only other sound was the gentle cool breeze every now and then rustling the leaves in the big gum tree.

BLACK AND STRONG

I was born Lavinia Kate Connell in May 1950, almost exactly in the middle of the twentieth century. Nothing extraordinary about that fact. But some of the things I have been through in my life might give you a better understanding and an appreciation of what it's like to be born an Aboriginal female in this place the world calls Australia.

I have to start with my parents because without them I would not be here. My mum was born in 1910. She is a Binjarib woman, a direct descendant of the original Nyoongar people from the Pinjarra area in the south-west of Western Australia. A Binjarib Nyoongar. We consider ourselves coastal plain people and we have a strong spiritual and cultural connection to both fresh water and salt water. Fresh water because we lived right near the bilyah, the river which flowed down from the hills to our east. Salt water because within walking distance of where we lived, the river emptied first into the estuary, then the ocean to the west. It was the perfect location for hunting and fishing throughout the year.

Our mob are the Binjarib traditional and custodial owners. Our ancestry can be traced through both our oral history and the recorded history of the wadjerlar colonists since settlement. It was Mum's people, my ancestors, who were killed by white soldiers at the massacre which took place in Binjarib country at Pinjarra in 1834.

Our stories and songlines, our sacred and special sites, and our very cosmology is deeply imbedded in our Binjarib language, land and cultural knowledge. My mum taught us her Binjarib Nyoongar language, but insisted we never spoke it at school. To the white authorities our language was the devil's own. We risked being taken away from our families if we were ever heard speaking it.

We loved listening to the yarns Mum told. She made us so proud that some of our people had survived the 1834 massacre. How our ancestors had come up against wadjerlar soldiers on horseback, with guns and swords when our maaman only had spears, koondees and boomerangs. Yet despite the overwhelming odds, with many of our people dying, there were those who had lived to pass on to our own children and grandchildren the stories and language for us to share the truth of what happened.

My mum was a very special woman. She was born in Nyoongar Boodja – Nyoongar country – the only sister with five brothers. Like my mum, my uncles passed the Binjarib stories on to their children as well. Of course, their recollections were from a male perspective, but the outcomes all tallied. Each one of her brothers loved Mum and treated her with utmost respect. I have never known any of my five uncles to have said even one angry word to their sister. Ever!

Mum was the keeper of our Binjarib history and stories, a very strong-minded woman, much loved and respected by all her family. Not even government policy could break the family bonds that existed between Mum, her husband, ten children and all her brothers.

One particular policy that really irked Mum related to the citizenship rights papers, as it was referred to among our family at the time. Those Aboriginal people who were given the papers were allowed to enter the pubs and buy alcohol. They were also permitted to be on the streets before the six o'clock morning curfew and after the six o'clock evening curfew. It gave them quite a bit of freedom to go about their business and they were seen as 'white citizens'. On the downside, anyone granted those papers was not allowed to interact or socialise with other Aboriginal people. Family members included. If caught doing so, they would lose their papers and face jail.

As Mum told us, 'I would never apply to get those papers. I have spent too much of my life being separated from my brothers. First, in New Norcia Mission, and then I was put in Moore River Native Settlement. My brothers and their families are worth more to me than being classified as a white person. I love my family so the government can keep their papers.'

Dad, too, was born in 1910, in the springtime. At least, that was the year the authorities estimated he came into the world. Dad was not a Nyoongar man. His mum, my paternal Nanna Mary, was a Palyku Mulbpa woman from around the Nullagine area. His father was a wayfaring Irishman. Dad was born in the Pilbara on the banks of the Shaw River at Hillside Station. The homestead was not far from Marble Bar, about seventy miles south-west of the small gold mining town, but it was more than nine hundred miles north of Perth. He was taken away from Nanna Mary and sent to Perth when he was very young, about eight years old.

Dad always told us that he first met Mum when he was living in Moore River Native Settlement. Mum had been sent to the same place from New Norcia Mission as a fourteen-year-old when she was deemed old enough to go out and work on the stations.

Although they were never sent to work at the same place, Mum and Dad told us it was really tough working on the stations. He cleared the land, put up fences, broke in horses, rounded up cattle and fixed windmills on the stations where he worked. Mum worked in various homesteads as a housemaid. She kept the homes clean and cooked all the meals for the station owners and their family, sometimes for ten or more people. The hours were long, from sunrise to sundown, and they were paid a pittance. But my mum and dad were survivors. And they always caught up with each other whenever they were sent back to Moore River Native Settlement if their work ran out on the stations.

As it turned out, government and religious rules proved to be hurdles to their plans for a long-term relationship. Back then, if Aboriginal people wanted to marry, they had to apply to the government, and their respective churches, for permission to do so. When my parents finally married in 1934, after years of red tape, they shared a whole lot of love, mutual respect, appreciation and tolerance for each other, and it endured over their years together.

As Dad often told us, 'I met the love of my life at Moore River Native Settlement when I was fourteen years old, back in nineteen twenty-four. From that day onwards, I knew your mother was the only one for me. I have never regretted marrying that beautiful girl.'

Theirs was a love story that lasted more than fifty years. Right up until he died in August 1992, many years after Mum, who passed away in 1975, he still proclaimed his love for her.

Apart from his own children and our mum, Dad had no other immediate family living around Pinjarra. From time to time he was visited by our people from up north. And though it was usually very late when they turned up, Dad always walked to our fence line to talk with them. Mum warned us kids not to stickybeak when we tried to sneak a glimpse of them standing out in the moonlight talking with Dad. From what I could barely hear, the men spoke in a language I couldn't understand. Mum said it was 'men's business'.

I realised later that us kids were multicultural even in our own country. Binjarib Nyoongar, Palyku Mulbpa and Irish. When tracing our family tree, very early mention is also made of an American ancestor who sailed here and married a Nyoongar woman from the Albany region. Another interesting fact Mum often told us was that her great-great-grandmother was of Chinese heritage. In the features of some of my siblings there is definitely a strong Asian influence.

Ancestry aside, to the Australian government back then we were classified as Aboriginal. Since colonisation, our people had been through some traumatic times with very limited freedom to do what we wanted. Even as adults, government policy dictated everything we did – and you will find this story is full of them. The rules applied to everyone, and authorities made sure they were diligently enforced. Our people had to be strong just to survive.

OUR OLD PLACE

There were some good times in my young life and my childhood was a happy one. There was Mum and Dad, four older sisters – Jane, Lucy, Verna and Rita – and four older brothers – Trevor, Jono, Edwin and Clem, before me. Then there was one little sister, Hannah, born after me. I was surrounded by family and never short of company. Mum's brother, Uncle Levi and his wife, Aunty May, and their family of nine children, including Gertie, Rhona and Claude, lived close by, so there were plenty of first cousins around.

Our families were always under the watchful eye of the local police. If our people wanted to travel to another place, for whatever reason, they had to check with the munartj. They had to tell them where and why they were going, if they would be staying with anyone and when they would be back. Should anyone not report their movements, they could be arrested. If they had children and that happened, the koolungahs could be forcibly removed.

Life was pretty tough for all Nyoongars, but Mum and Dad managed to make a good, safe home for their family. Soon after moving to Pinjarra – a sheep and dairy cattle farming district about fifty miles south of Perth – Dad found work clearing the land on various farms. At times he and Mum lived on the farms in sheds or makeshift dwellings. Other times they lived in tents. By 1950, just before I was born and after six years of moving from place to place, Dad had enough money saved to actually purchase a five-acre block of land. By hand, he cleared it of trees and bushland and built a three-bedroom house on it for his family.

Our home was made out of wooden upright planks with strong interior beams that supported a galvanised tin roof. The house itself was a pretty simple structure of three rooms, plus there was a passage down the centre with a kitchen area which had an open fireplace leading into a wide chimney.

We had no electricity or running water. In order to get light and fresh air inside, the windows were a hinged tin flap, pushed out and supported by a piece of wood to hold it open. There were two windows in the front and two windows at the back. To ensure our safety, each night the flaps were let down and tightly secured with a lock. Even during the day, if no one was home, the flaps would be shut tight. Our family didn't have fancy things, but Mum and Dad wanted to protect what we did have.

For the first few years, our house had a grey bare-earth floor that looked like it was made with compacted ant hills. Later Dad filled that area with cement. An open fire and kerosene lamps gave light at night-time. About eighty yards from the house there was a deep well, dug out by Dad and Uncle Levi, and that provided us with clean, clear water that was carted to the house in metal buckets. We never even heard of a fridge until our parents purchased a kerosene refrigerator. Before that, in order to keep our food cold, Mum used a lightweight metal cupboard, or 'meat safe', to hold the perishable food. It would be covered with wet hessian bags and suspended from a wooden beam in the house near a window, or even outside from a tree. Similar to a canvas water bag, whenever a breeze blew, it would cool the contents of the safe. Dad said it was a 'Coolgardie cooler'.

Television was a decade away but it made little difference to us because we didn't have electricity. We did listen to an old portable radio, but Dad mainly tuned into the parliamentary debates on the ABC radio broadcasts and that was boring to us kids. Mostly we read cowboy books or comics – *The Phantom* and *Adventures of Billy Bunter* – and the English *Women's Weekly* magazine that Mum ordered every week from the local newsagent.

An old outhouse, or goonamia, with a shit bucket, was built about three hundred yards from the house. Once full, the waste was taken another hundred yards further away by Dad, and later by my older brothers, and buried. Living conditions were pretty rough, but Dad and Mum managed to raise us ten kids right there on our property.

Along with Mum, Dad and us ten kids, we had a female dog named Gypsy, fifteen chooks and three geese. We also had a big vegie garden. Every autumn Mum planted different vegetables and some flowers and, come spring, we'd have the best Nyoongar garden in town.

The men in our family and our extended family had spears and fishing lines. Uncle Levi also had several big dogs for hunting kangaroos and rabbits. Sometimes the blokes walked for miles but they always came back with enough rabbit, possum and kangaroo meat for both families. Plus, Dad was always working and earning money and Mum made sure most of that went into paying the bills and keeping our cupboards full, so we hardly ever went hungry.

Because we were Nyoongars, the government decreed that the house and land could not be situated any closer than a mile from the local post office. No black person was allowed to own land or live any nearer than that to the post office in town. As youngsters, none of us kids knew about that rule or cared. We considered our family to be lucky, even though it meant a long walk to school and the shops if we needed anything.

My Uncle Levi and Aunty May had purchased a block of land just north of Dad's property and they looked after their family of nine children the same way. To me their house always seemed bigger than ours, with its extra rooms and a front verandah. Because it was close to our place, company was never far away. Uncle Levi was

Mum's oldest brother. She also had four younger brothers but she and Uncle Levi were really close. Being Nyoongars and kept under close and rigorous scrutiny by the government policies of the time, both had come through some very tough years in their early lives. And though Dad had five brothers-in-law, there was an obvious friendship between all of them.

At the time of my growing-up years, those same government policies, introduced soon after colonisation, still had an enormous impact on my parents' lives. In so many instances, those policies continued to dictate a lot how we kids were brought up by Mum and Dad, especially what we could and could not do. It was like all our Nyoongar families had to walk on tenterhooks in case it even seemed we might break some law related to us.

These polices created problems when our menfolk found jobs on farms and had to travel away from Pinjarra each day to get to them. A number of my uncles and older male cousins, who had to travel on the train to get to work before six in the morning, had to get special permission from the local sergeant. In those days, they often had to catch a ride on the goods train going through our town at four or five in the morning. They had to report their weekly whereabouts to the local munartj and get written approval for all their movements outside curfew hours.

Our men were not criminals, just hard-working blokes trying to earn some money to support their wives and children. Times were very hard for everyone in the 1950s, but it was made so much more difficult just because we were Aboriginal.

TOUGH TIMES

In those days, as long as I had my mum and dad, a feed and a bed, I was okay. But I have to tell you, there were periods in my life as a young Nyoongar girl that I found really hard going. To some I know it may sound petty, but back then it bothered me, especially when I got to an age where I began to notice things happening around me and I overheard comments by family and friends.

For instance, when people talked about who was the prettiest in our Connell family – and there being six sisters – my name always seemed to be last on the list. My older sisters with their pretty faces, perfect brown skin and long jet-black hair have won beauty contests. Rightly so. They were very beautiful. Glamorous photographs and huge beauty competition trophies attest to those facts.

My youngest sister, Hannah, much like our oldest one, Janie, has a natural Nyoongar and Asian-influenced beauty, with her black hair, dark doe eyes and smooth unblemished olive skin. But me? With my very pale skin, honey-blonde hair and hazel eyes, thanks to the genetic traits I inherited from my Irish grandfather, I seemed destined to miss out on the compliments. Especially from other Nyoongars.

When my brothers wanted to be extra mean to me, they said our mum had brought the wrong baby home from the hospital. I hardly ever got any compliments. Oh, I sometimes received a mention, but mainly because I was very good at sports and smart in school work. But as a young girl I always felt I missed out when the really pretty faces were handed out in heaven.

I know my mum loved me and she always said, 'Lavinia, it's not what you look like on the outside. It's whether you are a good person on the inside that counts. God is watching what we do, not what we look like. He already knows those details. So you remember that's how He will judge us. By our actions. Who cares what other people think? They just ordinary humans.'

My mum's words eased my mind. Still, at the time I always thought maybe I should have been the one called Jane. In my mind it surely was a match with me being plain.

There were other tough things about being a Nyoongar girl. And knowing how to fight was one of them, and it was going to come in useful throughout my life. When my four brothers had to fight five other boys, I always fought the boy who was about the same age as me. No hair pulling, biting or scratching like girls fight. It was stand back, shape up and punch each other. Queensbury Rules boxing, Dad said. Maybe if I wasn't such a tomboy and belted them up, those boys might have called me pretty.

Though I was never – and I am not now – a vain person, there were times when people commented on my appearance in a really spiteful way. It was so hurtful to be told, 'Lavinia, you wanna know something? From a distance, yeah, you looked gorgeous. But up close? Nah. Nah. You don't even look Nyoongar. Are you sure you're Aboriginal? You are so white.' Then the laughter.

When I was thirteen, this was said to me in front of a group of my peers. My two best friends got so angry with the person who said it, they wanted to punch into him. At the time I retorted by telling that bloke to get nicked. He apologised only because he was scared my friends wanted to hit him, but I could tell his apology was fake. Besides, his words were out and they couldn't be taken back. It stung. I realised later that I was angry for two reasons. One for being called ugly, but also it hurt more to be challenged about being a Nyoongar just because of the light colour of my skin. Thanks, Grandfather!

Another time, I was asked by an acquaintance if I was truly an Aboriginal and whether I should be talking about Nyoongar people. I turned and walked off, but not before I told him to go fornicate with himself with the old Queensland bush medicine, a big prickly pineapple.

I told that mean-mouthed bastard in both English and Nyoongar. Fortunately, that second time I was no longer a teenager. I was in my mid-twenties, yet it brought back a reminder of the days when I was younger and more vulnerable to mean comments like these.

Another painful memory as a youngster relates to government policy and its impact on our people. At any given time, it wasn't hard for the authorities to keep track of us Nyoongars. Especially those six families who owned land and were permanent residents in the town, like our family and Uncle Levi's. Because our land was near a big swamp, the police identified us as the 'Swampies'. There were also about seven other Nyoongar families living in the area, but they had all set up camps on reserved government land. They became known as the 'Reserve Mob'. They had found steady work on the farms and with government agencies, like the Public Works Department, and settled with their families in Pinjarra. In all, there must have been close to eighty Nyoongars in the town who had no intention of moving away.

Then there were transient families who only came to town for seasonal work and moved on when that ran out. They usually stayed with relatives for the duration and sent their little ones to the same state school we went to. Sometimes when that happened, the number of Nyoongar kids in the classes almost doubled. Some families also enrolled their children in the local Catholic school. Strict government rules said it was compulsory for all young Nyoongar kids to get educated. Rain, hail or shine. If we missed even one day, there had to be a note from Mum or Dad or one of the older sisters who had already left school. If there was no note, the police could be, and often were, contacted by the school and sent to check why we hadn't turned up.

There was one cardinal rule for every Nyoongar, whether you were transient or a permanent resident. If you were moving into town or leaving the place, you had to report your movements to the police. Failure to comply could mean jail for the parents and the forced removal of their children.

I remember when my first cousin Gertie, who was some twenty years older than me, had her six children taken away from her. Her oldest child, Margie, at eleven, was only a year older than me and Nina, the youngest, only six. Yet they were unceremoniously placed in a Catholic mission because she could not account for why her koolungahs were not at school. It didn't matter that she was heavily pregnant and needed help with other serious health issues. Or that her husband, Dan, had to travel away for weeks at a time shearing sheep for farmers in other towns so he could earn some money for his family.

Her children were attending the local Catholic primary school, so maybe they were under even closer scrutiny and monitoring by the convent nuns. More so than those of us at state school. I don't know the reason. I do know that it upset a whole lot of people in our Nyoongar community. Those six kids were an integral part of our family group. Everything changed when they were taken away by the government. Everybody grieved for them, it was so sad. We missed them terribly. It took a long time, especially for everyone in our close-knit families, to adjust to not having them around.

Even though they were allowed to come home during the summer for the school holidays, it was never, ever the same. Most people seemed to understand why their mother, after delivering her seventh baby, turned to alcohol to blot out the hurt of not having all her kids with her. Luckily other family members helped to rear the new baby. But as a one-year-old, that little boy was taken away too. It was a terrible time for everyone, especially us kids. Their departure hurt even more because we kids had spent a whole lot of our lives growing up with them. Then suddenly, they were gone.

We had all gone bushwalking together, hunting for kaardas (big yellow speckled goannas), rabbits, parrots, koomools (possums) and wild ducks. Picking wild berries. Pinching mulberries from the big tree in the middle of the wadjerlar neighbour's farm, running through the paddocks and being chased by big angry cows and bullocks.

We would spend nearly all our summer months together at the river swimming, fishing and catching marrons – fresh water crayfish. The river sustained us in so many ways. We not only had our bush tucker, but pinching the juicy grapes and ripe stone fruit – apricots, nectarines and peaches – from the orchards that grew near the river. As a last resort, there was always the nuts from the pine trees that grew alongside the Anglican church. Mum didn't like us eating those because it was said they caused rickets or some illness like that in kids.

And I remember a big mob of us kids crammed together on the back of my dad's old Model T Ford going to the estuary, crabbing and camping out. We rarely went alone, with other family members in their own vehicles forming a mini convoy of winyarn, rickety old trucks and motor cars heading out.

I clearly remember being taught what we could and couldn't eat from the bush, and all about our medicine plants. Making sure we tossed some sand into the river to let the spirits know we were there before we cast our fishing lines. Learning from our oldies about our culture and using our own language. We felt so special, having our own Binjarib words. Like some secret code that only we would know. Being reared in the mission, Mum and Dad would have never, ever allowed it, but in secret our older girl cousins taught us our Nyoongar swear words.

At home we were taught our Nyoongar language and culture. We learned that unlike the wadjerlars, who only had four seasons in a year, we had six. Biruk – when it is very hot in December and January; Bunuru – still hot but with the promise of cooler days in February and March; Djeran – cooler weather with signs of early rain in April and May; Makuru – when the heavy showers come down in June and July; Djilba – a time of new growth and flowers everywhere in August and September; and Kambarang – warmer sunny days around October and November. Our Elders explained that our bush medicines and our food supply depended on and varied with each of our seasons.

We were taught what signs to look for when hunting kangaroos, emus, goannas, possums and rabbits. The one thing our family was never allowed to eat was the booyaiy – long-necked turtle – because that was our totem. We spent so much of our time honing our bush skills. To us it was childhood heaven.

Sometimes we even packed some bread or dampa and cold meat from home and took it with us, along with a flagon of sweet black tea. That way we would stay at the river nearly all day. If any of us kids happened to have some money, we'd chuck in and buy a loaf of bread, chips, tinned meat or polony and a bottle of cool drink to share. There were even times when Mum let us book up at the local grocery store and paid the account on Dad's payday. Whenever that happened, a couple of packets of Granita biscuits was the favourite with all of us. Things were tough at times but we rarely went hungry or thirsty over summer because we all shared what we had. While in primary school, I remember reading about the adventures of Tom Sawyer and Huck Finn. Those two may have had the mighty Mississippi but they had nothing on us lot. We had the pure, clear waters of the Murray. It was like God himself had given us Nyoongars this special gift out of nowhere. Serendipity.

THE RESERVE

A few months after Gertie's children – Margie, Nina and their siblings – left for the mission, I became friends with some other Nyoongar kids in town. My best friend, Margie, was no longer around and I didn't know when she would be back. I knew who these others were because I had mixed with them at school. But they were the Reserve Mob and we Swampies had previously kept our distance.

However, one of Mum's best friends, Aunty Milly, lived on the reserve. She was a Yamatji woman from the Mid West region of Western Australia, who had married a Nyoongar man. The two women had been friends since they were young and with Aunty Milly being a person of sober habits, my mum trusted her with us kids. So, even though she lived on the reserve, we were allowed to stay with her. Aunty Milly would take care of us younger ones for a few days whenever Mum and Dad had business away from our town. Along with her kids, she would put us off to school. It never happened very often but Mum knew we would be safe there.

One of Aunty Milly's sons, Benjamin, was the same age as me, though a year behind me in school. He was one of the kids I started to mix with when Margie was taken away. I also made friends with two other reserve kids around my age – Leira Kagan and Cathy Bilson. Our parents didn't mind us hanging around together. After all, our mothers were friends and often played cards together.

My dad and Leira's dad both worked for the local Public Works

Department, digging and clearing the major drains and water channels in the district.

Staying with them on the reserve was so different from being in our own home. Aunty Milly's house was made from timber pieces, sheets of tin nailed together for the roof, hessian bags and canvas for the walls, and bits of old carpet covered the bare floor.

Only one or two homes were similar to ours with timber walls and a tin roof. But like so many other reserve homes, Aunty Milly's was more or less a humpy because most of it had been built from materials found at the local rubbish tip.

Everyone had shared access to running water and there was a big ablution block built about a hundred yards away. The government had put it up for them to use. There was one side for females and the other for males. We young ones were never allowed to go to that ugly, grey building without an adult family member. Everybody on the reserve used them.

Aunty Milly and her family had to get their water from that same tap and cart it back to their house in buckets. Sometimes there was a line up because there were about six other families that got water from that one government tap.

With no electricity at Aunty Milly's, the big Tilley lamp would be filled with kerosene and lit just on sunset to provide light right throughout the night. Yet like our place, her mia-mia was always clean, warm and fairly comfortable. And we never, ever went hungry.

I remember very clearly, if the weather was hot, Aunty Milly would pay us one shilling each if we caught a kaarda for her to eat. She would toss the big lizard straight on the coals and cover it lightly with hot ashes. Once cooked, it would be taken out and left to cool. Aunty Milly never waited too long because she liked to eat the white meat even while it was still hot. 'Land fish', she called it, and made sure we all had a taste, but each time she had the first and biggest serve. Two things Aunty Milly never ate were the yornah – the blue-tongue goanna – and the yuntarn – a big, black poisonous goanna. If we brought them back to her place, she would just chuck them away or give them to the dogs.

Everyone who knew Aunty Milly knew she was one tough Yamatji woman and no one messed with her. She could count, but couldn't read or write and would always sign her name on government papers with a cross. Her word was enough for everyone else, including the local white people. She knew about numbers and particularly money. She had no problem coping with the conversion to the decimal currency when the government introduced it in the 1960s and pounds, shillings and pence became dollars and cents. Aunty Milly learned it all. She knew about boya.

She loved her card games and would have a game of rummy once or twice a week with the other Nyoongar women in town, especially around the workers' paydays. Only adult women could join in, and Elders were always given a place at the table before anyone else. If there was no table, the ladies would all sit on a blanket on the ground. They made sure to select a place in the shade and out of the wind. They would sit for hours without moving, often sending us kids to the shops to buy bread, cold meat and soft drinks for them and us.

Occasionally we kids were allowed to sit and listen to the funny yarns being told by the card players. But if there was something really serious or some juicy gossip to be talked about, we were not allowed to listen in at all. At those times we kids were told in no uncertain terms to go and play somewhere else or get a hiding.

When I look back, I reckon those card schools contributed to part of our Nyoongar economy. They certainly formed an integral part of our community. It was a chance for the women to get together and yarn with each other and share family news. It also gave them a chance to win some money to buy food if they were struggling. In some ways it was funny, because after nearly every game, losers borrowed some money from the winners and paid it back next game. The card games weren't always plain sailing. Now and again some woman would challenge another if they had a gripe with them. The other card players quickly told them to settle down or get on their way.

A couple of times, some women would get into a fist fight. If they didn't sort it out or if things got too violent, someone would run and get the munartj, much to everyone's disappointment. The threat of police coming around put an immediate stop to the card game. Along with a whole lot of other laws relating to our people, it was illegal for us Nyoongars to gamble for money in their homes and the adults risked jail if they were caught. Sometimes those troublemakers were banned from playing cards or two-up ever again, especially if the munartj had to be called. Their unruly behaviour disrupted what was usually a friendly, social pastime for a lot of Nyoongars and was especially disappointing for those players who had been winning.

CONFIRMATION

It was around that time a few of our Nyoongar mothers were employed as housekeepers and cooks for local white families. My mum worked for Lady McLarty at their Pinjarra residence, Edenvale. Lady McLarty was the wife of Sir Ross McLarty, the then premier of Western Australia. There was a definite prestige attached to Mum's position and our family benefitted in more ways than one from that connection.

It was with encouragement from Lady McLarty and other prominent wadjerlar families that Leira Kagan, Cathy Bilson and I did Bible study with the Anglican Church and got confirmed. There was no way Benjamin was going to be a part of that, being a Nyoongar Yamatji boy and all. According to him that was girls' stuff.

A requirement of getting confirmed was once a week we girls did some Bible study after school with the Sunday school teacher. It also meant we had to go to church every Sunday for three months straight. It was quite a big deal for our Nyoongar families, studying the Bible, going to church regularly and finally getting confirmed. Of course, it was all voluntary on our part. We three girls were lucky. Not like when Mum was growing up in New Norcia Mission and they had Bible teachings and prayers forced on them.

Well, confirmation day finally arrived. Not all my relatives could come because some of them were nursing hangovers from Saturday night. And my uncles said no self-respecting Catholic should step into an Anglican church. Ever! But both Mum and Dad were in church that Sunday and, for me at least, it turned out to be a very interesting day.

Like all the wadjerlar kids getting confirmed that Sunday, we Nyoongar girls had to get dressed all in white, including wearing a small veil and white shoes and socks. Somewhat nervously Leira, Cathy and I took our first Holy Communion.

The church was packed as we sat in the front row pews. When our turn came, us newly confirmed Nyoongar girls stood and walked nervously down to Reverend Bromile to be blessed. Lambs to the slaughter. I went first. The preacher placed the holy bread on my tongue. Like eating thin dampa. That went well enough. Then he tipped the goblet up to my innocent lips to give me a sip of the holy sacrament. It was the first time I had ever tasted wine. Kgaepa. I very nearly choked! It was sweet, but it burnt my throat.

With that one sip I felt totally confused, even guilty. Although Mum and Dad, my older brothers and extended family had all indulged in boozing from time to time, drinking any sort of alcohol was absolutely taboo for us kids. As well, we Nyoongars were banned by government policy from buying and drinking alcohol unless we had those Citizenship Rights papers. We could be jailed for doing it. Yet here I was, a young girl in church, the holiest of all holy places for wadjerlars, being given wine by the local preacher. Their Anglican man of God! And with our parents' approval and blessing! My head was in a spin.

Not long after being confirmed, Leira, Cathy and I were also invited to join the local Girl Guides troop. Most of the other wadjerlar girls in the group went to our school and the Guides' leader was the mother of one of my school mates. Similar to getting confirmed, this too involved a bit of study but it was very much a practical, hands-on learning experience.

Following our Christian confirmation, it looked like our souls would be saved once we drank the holy wine every Sunday. But with the Girl Guides, it was physical challenges that were put to us and we readily took them on. We had a wicked lot of fun. There was always plenty of laughter and I really enjoyed becoming a fully fledged member. Putting up a tent, tying a multitude of knots, and in case of an accident, running one mile to save a life were some of our challenges.

We had to cook over an open fire and it was a cinch because in our home that's how we cooked all our meals all year round anyway. We three Nyoongar girls passed every Girl Guide test hands-down. We even attended a bush camp in the hills overlooking the city not far from Lesmurdie.

But for me, the highlight was getting dressed in our blue Girl Guide uniforms and marching in the local Anzac parade in the main street, right alongside a bloke wearing a tartan skirt and playing Scottish bagpipes. To me, the sound was amazing.

As with our confirmation, there was also a bit of fanfare when we got out first uniforms. We had to pose moorditj way because we had our photos taken for the local newspaper and the latest Department of Native Welfare news booklet. After all, as we were told by our parents, we three black girls were breaking new ground by being some of the first Nyoongars in Western Australia to become Girl Guides.

In between getting confirmed and becoming Girl Guides, a lot of our spare time was spent together in a group with Benjamin, my younger cousin Ricky and Leira's younger brother, Tedo. We never wanted them following us around but our oldies told us the boys had to come along too, or we couldn't go. They could be really annoying sometimes but mostly, if the weather was hot, we all just went swimming. Otherwise we spent time together walking around our small town, running errands for our parents and going to school.

If there was cricket or a footy match and our brothers were playing, we'd always meet up together there. Except for Ricky, those in our little group were not related to me. They became my best friends though, and filled the empty space that had been left when the Native Welfare took my cousin Gertie's children away and put them in the mission.

HOLIDAY TIME

When we did finally catch up with Margie, Nina and the others, things had definitely changed for all of us. We were all a bit older. Like me, they had made new friends too. Margie now had more in common with her new friends and seemed to relate better to the other mission kids. Being closely related, we still spent some good family times together. Everyone was so happy when they came back home, talking about all the new stuff they had learned. Telling us every little thing they were taught by the nuns and how their lives were now being run like clockwork. All they talked about was school, keeping their dormitories neat and tidy and the many prayers they had to recite perfectly for the nuns. We all laughed when they found out I had been going to church and had been confirmed as well. One of them said it was a good thing, because even though I wasn't Catholic, my soul would most likely end up in heaven too.

There were other times though when we got really quiet and serious. Mostly when we were sitting around a big open fire after swimming all day. The stories they told us then were not so pretty. Particularly when they described the various types of harsh punishment the kids got if their tasks were not done properly. Or when they could not recite the prayers attached to each rosary bead. The oldest girl was only eleven, yet she and her younger sisters all got a flogging with a leather strap from the nuns if they messed up at all. I felt really sorry for them. Especially hearing about the beatings, and because being placed in the mission was through no fault of their own. And now the Native Welfare and Catholic mission only allowed them to come home for the holidays.

Something happened during one of their summer breaks from the mission and it stays in my mind even today. It was around Christmas time and they had been home from the mission about a week. Mum said it was okay for me to have a sleepover with Margie and her sisters at Gertie's house.

As usual after supper, all us kids sat around the big log fire outside telling yarns and ghost stories. We had been given a feed of kangaroo stew, dampa and black sweet tea for supper, followed by slices of a big ripe watermelon from Uncle Levi's garden. Because we had spent the day at the river it wasn't long before some of us were nodding off. My cousin Gertie told us to go settle down for the night because she and her husband, Dan, were walking over to her mum and dad's place to have a quiet drink. The oldies' place was only about a hundred yards away from us kids but still within shouting distance and it was one of the few times that Dan, a gun shearer, was not away at work.

I'm not too sure how long we had been asleep, but we were suddenly awakened by the three dogs barking and a car pulling up just down the road. We heard a car door shut, a few giggles interspersed with two muffled voices saying their goodnights. The vehicle then took off, engine roaring. A few minutes later my cousin Rhona came in giggling and trying not to make too much noise. We could smell a faint hint of lavender essence on her clothes. Lavender was the perfume of the time and she must have pinched some from her sister Gertie. Uncle Levi was pretty strict about young girls growing up too fast, using make-up and wearing perfume, and we knew she couldn't afford it herself.

Anyway, Rhona started to undress, changed her mind and, still fully dressed, hopped into bed next to her little niece. That night we were all sleeping on a big double bed. I was nearest to the wall, Margie in the middle next to me and Nina the baby sister sleeping in the front. Rhona squeezed into bed next to little Nina and was soon fast asleep and snoring.

I must have gone to sleep too because next minute I heard her whispering loudly, telling someone to get out. I froze. It was a man and he was lying on top of Rhona on the bed, so we couldn't see his face. He was telling her to open her legs. Rhona told him to get off her as she tried to push him away and wriggle out of his grasp.

He slapped her hard and I clearly heard him whisper back, 'If you don't, I will do this with the young bitch lying next to you. I will stick her real good. You want that, slut?'

The threat of her seven-year-old niece being harmed was too great. My cousin Rhona, who by this time had started to cry, whispered to him to go lie on the floor with her. Although she was scared for herself, she would do whatever the bastard wanted as long as he left little Nina alone.

I elbowed Margie to see if she was awake. She nudged me back. Through the soft light provided by Gertie's Tilley lamp we could see the man and a terrified Rhona get off the bed. She must have been moving too slow for him because he roughly shoved her down onto the floor. Really hard. He slapped Rhona's face again with such force she groaned and I saw a trickle of blood come from her mouth.

He then ripped her skirt and top open. He unzipped his trousers. Then, forcing her legs open, he got on top of her. We heard Rhona's sharp, short scream, then another hard whack when the man hit her face again. She suddenly went very quiet. Maybe she was knocked out or biting on her knuckles so as not to scream again, but the man was grunting like a pig as he pounded her body with his own. We could smell the overwhelming stench of alcohol on him.

I was ready to bolt. I started to move, to get up, but Margie, being older and stronger than me, held me back, shaking her head from side to side. 'No, no, no,' she mouthed. I slipped back under the blanket. I was so scared I wanted to piss myself.

By this time, we three girls in the bed were wide awake but we dared not move a muscle, not scarcely breathe. Then we heard him say out loud, 'I love your black cunt. That cold white bitch I married is useless. You black sluts, you all got fire down there, and I love that.'

We froze. We all recognised that man's voice. Margie was right to hold me back. With tears streaming down my face, I put my fist in my mouth for fear he might start on one of us if we made a sound. *It was like Satan himself had come into this house.*

With a final loud grunt, he finished with Rhona. After a brief slump, he roughly pushed her broken body aside and stood up and straightened his clothes. Before he left, he said, 'If you say anything to anyone at all, you know what will happen to you. If you say one single word about this next time it will be them young little black bitches laying there. So keep your poxy black mouth shut. You got that?'

Rhona just lay there, beaten and unable to move.

After the man slunk out the house, we could hear her sobbing before she pulled the coat around herself. She stayed on the hard floor. With fear pounding in our heads, we barely heard that second car start up and take off. That engine purred softly. Sneaking away in the darkness of night like slimy frog shit in a winter swamp.

Still shaking with fright, Margie tried to get up and bar the door, but Nina clung to her, making it difficult. I reached across and grabbed Nina, who was shaking badly. Trying to hide my own fear, I cuddled her bony frame close to me. Margie jumped up and barred the door.

Margie said if their parents came home, they could just knock. Only then would she let them in. Margie asked Rhona if she was okay, but got nothing in reply. In the muted glow we could see the tears still streaming down her face mingling with blood from her battered lips and nose. Dark bruises were appearing on her swollen cheeks. Rhona whispered for us to go back to sleep and forget what had happened – as if that would ever be possible. In that moment, it felt as if our childhood, our innocence, had been smashed by what we had witnessed.

Daylight was creeping through the window before any of us moved. It must have been about an hour or more that we had been lying there sleepless and shocked. I stirred the other two girls up and we helped Rhona get onto the bed. After covering her with the blankets, and promising to get help we crept out the door and took off to my place. We had no shoes on and it was freezing cold but we kept running as fast as we could, not even stopping at Uncle Levi's house. I wanted to get home to safety. To my mum.

Even though it was very early, as usual Mum and Dad were already up and about, making breakfast. Dad was cutting wood for the old stove before carting a bucket of water from the well. Mum was setting up a big pot of porridge to feed everyone. It sat alongside the old iron kettle filled with water for their first cup of tea.

In a cheery voice Mum asked, 'You girls getting around very early. What, did one of you piddle the bed or something?' I couldn't help myself. Tears started to flow down my cheeks and I began to sob as I told Mum what had happened. As she listened to us, shock gave way to silent tears for her niece.

Then Mum said, 'Where she now? Does she need a doctor? I'll go and see her and we'll go straight down and tell that new sergeant about this. He has to do something. Rhona's only fifteen. That bloke raped her. Oh, my poor niece. You poor babies.'

All three of us girls looked at each other.

I said, 'You can't do that Mum.'

'Why the bloody hell not, Lavinia?' Mum never, ever swore like that when talking to any of her children, especially us kids. But she was so angry and upset right now.

'Mum. It was the new sergeant. He's the bloke who did that to her. The sergeant punched into Rhona, then he raped her.'

My mum's face turned grey with shock. 'That dirty, filthy white bastard,' she shouted. 'The dog! And he supposed to be protecting us Nyoongars, the mongrel. God curse him.'

Then, seeing our traumatised faces, Mum lowered her tone. 'You girls wash your faces and get yourselves a feed. There's porridge already cooked and after that you can go and lay down on me and Dad's bed if you still tired. Old boy, grab your tea, let's go outside. We gotta help Rhona first, then we'll go and talk with Levi and May.'

After that, I was never allowed to stay overnight with the girls again. During their time at home on holidays, they could come and stay at our house. Whenever there was any boozing going on with their family, Mum insisted the young ones come over and stay for the night with us. It meant we all slept crowded together on the hard cement floor on thin kapok mattresses, but at least we were all safe.

It wasn't until about three months later, just before they had to go back to the mission, we girls heard that my young cousin had been taken away to a Catholic home for wayward girls in Perth. Cousin Rhona was just fifteen. She was nearly twelve weeks pregnant.

As the local Protector of Aborigines representative, the new sergeant had recommended to the court that she be sent away. After all, she was a bad influence on the community. There would be no punishment handed to him for bashing and raping her. I don't even know if any authority was ever told of his involvement. Not that it would have mattered with that bastard. Back in those days, we Nyoongars had no say. Our women and girls had even less. We were the bottom rung on society's ladder. And after all, he was the government authority in our town. Never mind he was also a rapist of our black females. He was the Munartj. The Sergeant. The Birrdier. The Big Boss. Our designated Protector.

In contrast, to the white people in our community, my cousin Rhona was seen as a stupid young Nyoongar girl who had gotten herself pregnant. Rhona had to be removed. Like so many other young black women and girls, that day in court Rhona became a victim all over again.

SPORT

Mum and Dad always insisted that getting educated was a top priority for us kids. And we did. By working hard in class and doing our homework every evening with the big Tilley light being put to good use. If we had no kerosene, Mum always kept candles on hand. I tried hard and got really good marks for my work, especially when doing our end of year exams. Each time I was promoted to the next class. Often both Mum and Dad joined in when we young ones had our family quiz nights. They asked us questions about everything from geography, mathematics and history to spelling. We even learned about the Ten Commandments and other texts from the Bible. It made learning fun and put us in good stead in the classroom.

But as a young girl, I was also lucky enough to be a gifted athlete. I won many school certificates for running, long jump and other track and field events. From Grade 1 to Grade 7, I took off the prize for champion girl for my age group every year. I was also a very good netball and softball player. In those times no Nyoongar had even heard of basketball. Even for the wadjerlars, those who had an inkling, believed it was strictly a game Americans played. Like baseball. In our little town, it was netball and softball for the girls, and football and cricket for the boys.

At home, I had plenty of practice playing those games. With four brothers in front of me, I strived to compete with them – especially my youngest brother, Clem, or Shorty, as he was called. The older brothers were too big and strong for me to beat, but I managed to give Clem a run for his money. I must have been okay because he always picked me on his team whenever us kids played rounders, cricket or skittles or any of the other team sports against other Nyoongar kids. Even the game brandi, where we risked getting stung by a tennis ball being thrown hard and fast straight at us.

Shorty would always be captain and he would pick Claude, our first cousin, and then me. Sometimes if Claude was on the other team, or not there at all, I would be Shorty's first choice.

Maybe Mum and Dad had told him he had to pick me or get a hiding. I would have dobbed on him if he did leave me out, but he never let me or Mum and Dad down. I always had a spot on his team.

There were times when Shorty and I competed against each other, but at those times Mum and Dad were usually present. Especially where running races were involved. Dad used to line us kids up at the start of the race according to age. Using Dad's reasoning and calculations, I always was given a few yards head start because I was three years younger than Clem, four years younger than Claude and five years younger than Edwin. No one could beat Jono who was too old to compete against us younger ones. Anyway, he was just too fast.

We had to run over three different distances: fifty yards, seventy-five yards and one hundred yards. Dad would step it out between our place and Uncle Levi's. We would start near the bog and finish at our house. If and when I beat Clem home, my brother would start shouting and complaining to Mum that Dad was showing favouritism to me by giving me too much of a start.

Starting from a level pegging, most times Clem would beat me, but when we raced according to Dad's rules, my brother couldn't catch me. There were times when I won our homegrown races and he would punch me at the end of it. To avoid being hit, and for my own protection, it got so I ran straight past the finish line over to where Mum, Dad or my oldest brothers, Trevor and Jono, were standing. I would duck behind them. Then it would be like the fox and the goose, with Shorty trying to clobber me for beating him past the post.

Apart from that threat, running those races was a lot of fun, especially when I beat both Clem and Claude. Cousin Claude couldn't really run fast at all even though he was taller than both Clem and me. He would lope along at the start but once he built up a bit of speed, he could stride out like a waitj in full flight being chased by kangaroo dogs. Too bad his built-up speed came at the same time the race was over. There was another reason why I ran so fast. The dogs. Uncle Levi had three big kangaroo dwerts, Laddie, Boy and Pally, and they were used for hunting. They would get all excited and agitated when we practised our running. What with all the shouting and measuring distances there was a lot of activity and noise. The dogs wanted to get in on the action too.

Well, they had no hope of catching me. The thought of those big dwerts with their huge sharp teeth snapping after me was enough to make me just about fly. I was glad to get past our gate because Gypsy, our female dog, let no other dog into our yard. Once I got past her, I knew I was safe from them. Those kangaroo dogs never came near Gypsy even though they were bigger, stronger and uglier than her. I don't know if the dogs made the other kids run faster, but they sure spurred me on.

All the racing we did around home made me into a good athlete at school. I loved competing and I loved my sport. When I was in Grade 5 and again in Grade 6, I got picked to play in our primary school's netball team. Ordinarily that team was always made up of Grade 7 girls only. I was an exception. Then, as a Grade 7 student, I was brought from primary school to play in the Pinjarra Junior

High School netball team. That had never happened before to any student, Nyoongar or wadjerlar. Mum and Dad were very proud and pleased when Mr Hamilton, our primary school headmaster, let them know.

The other athletic achievement I was happy about was having my name included on the honour board for Senior Girls Champion when I reached my third year in high school.

I had been champion girl in both my first and second years in high school – continuing on from Grade 7 in primary school – but I was extra proud to have my name included on the Pinjarra Junior High School honour board. To be champion girl, I had to win every individual event in which I competed.

This included the one-hundred-yard and two-hundred-yard sprints; the one-hundred-yard hurdles and cross-country running. In addition, I had to win the shot-put, discus throwing and both the high jump and long jump.

I won every event. My name was put on the honour board and it sets a record that cannot be broken, because in February the following year all Australia made the conversion to decimals. My eight events will stand forever now. In the history of our local high school, I was the first and only Nyoongar person to ever be the Senior Girls Sports Champion. I know I made Mum, Dad and my family proud that day. Especially my brother Trevor, who used to come and barrack for me at every sports carnival that I competed in over my years in school. As a young single bloke, Trev had a permanent job with one of the local farmers. He would borrow his boss's farm ute and come watch the interschool competitions.

I was very lucky that my parents and siblings, and even our extended family, encouraged my involvement in different types of sport. For instance, I always had good enough sandshoes and socks for netball, although most times the shoes were second-hand. But Mum always insisted we wear new socks and undies. These would be purchased brand new from Taylor's big all-purpose shop in Pinjarra. And Mum and my older sisters always made sure I could also get the correct uniforms for school or weekend netball. Somehow my parents always raked up enough money so I could buy something to eat after the games as well. Other times, Trev and Jono would chuck in some of their wages too. I really enjoyed my sports and I learned about teamwork and winning and losing. Mum and Dad instilled in us kids that we should enjoy what we were doing and try our hardest. Win, lose or draw.

Dad used to say, 'Nothing wrong with losing, as long as you give it your best shot. You do that and you're a winner anyway.' At the time I couldn't see the logic, but it sounded good when he said it.

Sometimes if the school sports carnival or netball carnival was local and we had no money, Mum would pack a picnic lunch of dampa, cold meat, boiled eggs, boiled whole potatoes and sweet tea and come and watch us kids.

Every time, there would always be a bit extra because some Nyoongar kids' parents never ever came to watch their children, or provide them with tucker either. So we shared with them whatever Mum had brought for us.

I was in high school now, but it still felt like a carefree time for us Nyoongar kids. We enjoyed going bush every chance we got, sometimes walking miles for a swim at a different spot on the river. Even the Bend never seemed too far and we could always cadge a ride back to town from my Uncle Mart who lived right near the Bend.

There were other changes happening too. Everybody was growing taller and our body shapes were developing differently. I got my first bra quite early into the school year and had the 'girls talk' from Mum and my older sisters.

My friend Ben had no qualms about telling us girls that he had begun to sprout hair on different parts of his body. We didn't want to know and told him to shut up. We could see for ourselves the fluff beginning to grow on his face, but it was not right for him to be telling us those things. I sometimes wonder if that was one of the reasons Ben left before the end of that year – so he didn't have to shave before school. We girls too were changing. We were beginning to look more rounded and shapely, but we still had our tomboy ways. At nearly thirteen, our bodies might have looked more mature, but our minds were still young and innocent in so many ways.

JUNIOR HIGH

One good thing to happen when I went to Pinjarra Junior High, was Margie also started in the same year as me. After they were taken back to the mission it wasn't until almost three years later those kids were allowed to return to live with their parents full-time. Margie's dad had gotten steady work close to home and her mum was really trying to be a good mother, getting the kids into some sort of routine. She was cooking and cleaning and only have a social drink on payday. And she rarely smoked, unlike so many other Nyoongars.

I was glad to have another Nyoongar person in high school with me. And because it was someone I was as close to as Margie, it made it fun and a bit easier to cope with the transition from primary school. Most of the other Nyoongar kids who were in primary school with me had either dropped out of school, or like Leira, been sent to study at a private boarding school in Perth. Others, like Cathy Bilson, had either left town with their families or had gone to work.

Thanks to Mum and Dad's insistence that we did our homework every night, and their twenty questions quizzing us about everything from geography and history to general knowledge, mathematics and spelling, we learned a lot. So I had made really good grades in primary school. Also, while in Grade 7, I was very fortunate to have our principal Mr Hamilton as my teacher. He made learning so interesting, easy to understand what was being taught and sometimes even fun. He always encouraged us Nyoongar kids to do better than we had ever done before. We tried hard not to let him down.

As a result of all the family testing us kids with quizzes and all the homework, combined with Mr Hamilton's teaching and encouragement, I was put into '8A' in my first year in high school. No Nyoongar kid had ever achieved such good results in the Grade 7 primary school tests to enter junior high school going into the class for top students.

But the teachers at junior high school thought I had cheated and demanded that I do another test. They believed I shouldn't, or couldn't, possibly be placed into '8A' in high school. I was Aboriginal, after all.

They made the mistake of contacting Mr Hamilton, my teacher and the headmaster of my primary school, to get his thoughts on the matter. He hit the roof. He told them straight out that the marks I got were my own. He had supervised the tests himself and told them he had taught me during Grade 7, so he knew my academic capabilities.

Despite them talking with Mr Hamilton, I was made to sit the high-school entry test again. This time I was the only student in the classroom along with two teachers. One sat with me for the duration of the test. The other left but checked in every ten minutes to see if everything was okay. When the time was up, I handed my papers to the teacher who checked that I had finished everything. She thanked me and said I could go to my next lesson.

A few days later I was called into the headmistress's office. I thought I was in real trouble for sure. I racked my brain trying to remember what I might have done wrong. To my surprise, Mrs Foster welcomed me in and said she had some news for me.

'Congratulations, Lavinia, your test results came back. I am so pleased to let you know that your marks this time were even higher than the first test you took with everyone else.' Appearing quite puzzled she shook her head and added, 'I really don't know why you had to repeat the entry test. Some teaching staff were doubtful about the original result, I suppose. However, this time, young lady, you got ninety-four per cent all up. Last time you only got ninety. Well done.'

I just about floated back to my home room. Such praise from Mrs Foster for any student was a rare thing indeed and I guess for a Nyoongar girl was unheard of. I couldn't wait to tell my family.

Mum, forever the realist, slightly took the edge off the good news and brought me back to earth when she said, 'I reckon that Mrs Foster is a pretentious old witch. If you ask me she was probably the one who insisted you take the test again in the first place. Blaming other teachers, my foot. Still, Lavinia we're very proud of the marks you got, my girl.'

NEW RULES

After that, I enjoyed my first year in high school. The whole subject structure was a bit confusing at first. Unlike in primary school, where every student did the same subject together, now we had a couple of options. Once I got used to the timetable, I was happy enough to attend. My brother Clem had gone through first and second years at this school before me, but he never talked to me about the differences I would find at high school.

Neither of my parents had experience with secondary school learning. Dad only went to Grade 3. Mum had been placed in New Norcia Mission, so she stayed at school until Grade 6. Both of them told us that once they got big enough physically, they had to go out to work for a living. So except for me and Clem, all my older sisters and brothers had gone to Perth to complete high school. The Native Welfare Department had provided hostels for them to board at during the school year and they only came home during the holidays. Once they graduated they went straight into work or further training, so we never did talk about me going into high school and what I might expect.

One thing I couldn't get used to was the fact that we had to wear a uniform every day. We had worn our Girl Guides uniforms and knew the importance of that symbol of belonging, but that was only on Friday evenings and weekends. In high school, it was compulsory to wear the school uniform every day. No more just chucking on any clean skirt and top and heading to the classroom like in primary school. To make it worse, we had to wear polished, black lace-up shoes and the correct light-blue socks.

We girls had to wear a school beret, tie, gloves and in winter, horrible thick grey stockings if we had to attend any public event.

Mrs Foster was always reminding us, 'Lavinia and Margie, you both are representing your school and you must always be aware of that. How you present yourself in public will reflect on you and your school and your family. So look smart there, young ladies.'

Margie and I caught up every lunch break. One day she told me she was thinking of leaving school when the August holidays rolled around. I was pretty shocked, but remembered she was older than me. And like most of the other Nyoongar kids who had been in Grade 7 with me last year and had already left, she was now planning to leave school too. With the majority of them being around fourteen years old, the government didn't seem to care one way or another. Some of them had found work and saw no reason to continue at school.

They knew how to read and write and sign their names with more than a cross on the dotted line, as many of our aunts, uncles and older cousins were doing. Plus, their families could always use the extra money brought in by working kids. When times were tough, it meant the difference between having food on the table and going hungry. Anyway, some of the oldies thought too much learning only gave us young ones stupid ideas. In their minds, too much white fullas' education would make us young ones think and act like we were better than every other Nyoongar.

Thank God Mum and Dad did not think like that. They encouraged us to get a good education. They always said it was the only way to cope in the white man's world. At home, Mum still made sure we learned our Nyoongar language and all about our Binjarib culture and family history. And our girl cousins still kept us abreast of the Nyoongar swear words, even inventing a few new ones when they got angry. However, we were warned every day never to use our language at school or to speak any Nyoongar words where the teachers or any white person would hear.

I managed to talk Margie into staying at least until the end of the school year. But knowing I might be the only Nyoongar kid left in high school the following year, I made friends with a few of the white kids in my class. One or two lived in town with their families but most of them came from Fairbridge Farm School and we could only ever be friends while attending school.

They were a mixed bunch of Brits who were brought out to Australia from the United Kingdom. Mum told us they were like us Nyoongars in some ways. Their government had forcibly removed them from their families too and had shipped them to Australia to help work on the farms.

They lived on a farm similar to a government-run Aboriginal mission and seemed to live under the same rules and regulations Margie and her siblings told us about in the Catholic mission when they were taken away.

Life at Fairbridge was very controlled. My friends had to work hard every weekend and after school. Some told me it was slave labour because they were never paid for any work they did. So apart from going to high school in Pinjarra, the Fairbridge kids were confined to the farm. Their work, religion, schooling and any social life they may have had revolved around that place.

For some reason, I got on really well with the Irish kids who attended high school with me. I got on better with them than the Aussie wadjerlars I had first met when I started primary school. Unlike the local white kids, the Irish never called us black niggers and they got angry with anyone who did call us Nyoongars insulting names.

DJURRIPIN

It was in my first year at high school that I experienced my first crush on a boy. He came from Fairbridge and I thought he was so good-looking. The first time I took any notice of him was when we collided on a corner in the school corridor. I was carrying some books and loose papers and they scattered everywhere when he bumped into me. I was just about to swear at him in Nyoongar when he apologised and helped me gather my papers.

Then he smiled at me. That was it. My thirteen-year-old heart flipped. I couldn't talk. He had the most beautiful eyes. His skin was darker than nearly everyone else from Fairbridge. In fact, in our whole school. I just nodded and walked away.

Gobsmacked! I was shaken right up. What the hell! Here was I, the toughest girl in the school bar none, feeling all flustered just because that boy had smiled at me. I must be sick. I was on the verge of being fourteen and should have had more sense. So why was I djurrupin, smiling, all the way to class?

I found out his name, that he was in his third year at high school and that he was Irish. Of course he was Irish! Whenever we passed in the corridor, in the common quadrangle area outside the classrooms or at sports practice, he would nod and smile at me.

That was it! His bumping into me was a serendipitous moment for sure. I must have started daydreaming straight away even though he had not spoken to me at all since he apologised.

At home my usual boisterous tomboy manner was replaced by something totally out of character. To everyone's surprise, the girl her brothers had nicknamed 'Lumberjack' and 'Luigi' started walking around humming, listening to every love song on the radio. I hung on every word sung by The Beatles. I even started doing whatever Mum asked me, without question. Suddenly, I cared about what I looked like.

Whether I was too fat, if my hair was okay and if I looked alright in my school uniform. My school uniform, for God's sake! Everyone dressed the same in that blue and maroon uniform. We were not allowed to wear make-up, so that was out. But I made sure my pleated uniform was ironed perfectly, even though I had to use the old fire-heated clothes iron.

Although we had no electricity or running water in our home, every day my hair was washed and shining and there was not one strand out of place. I had to get up early and cart a bucket of water from the well to heat up, but I didn't see that as a problem. All of a sudden I had changed from an all-out tomboy into what my brothers now called a 'stupid girl'. For the first time ever, I even felt pretty.

In a big family you can't keep anything secret for too long. My so-called best friend, Margie spilled the beans, telling my brother Clem that I had a crush on a boy in our high school. To make matters worse, Clem, who had only just left school at the start of his third year there, knew the boy. They had been in the same class together. Clem gave a number of reasons why this bloke was not a good choice for me. The main one being that he was a wadjerlar. They can't be trusted. It was spelt out loud and clear by my brother that colour prejudices can go both ways. He threatened to go there after school and punch the boy's head off. My crush was crushed then and there in an instant. After that, school didn't have the same appeal. Oh, he still looked my way all the time and once he even waved out. I just turned away. I didn't want him to get smashed by Shorty.

TRUANTS

A few months after Clem and Margie crushed my crush, I started ducking school. Margie and I would get dressed in our uniforms, pack our lunches and leave for school every morning. Instead of going to school we would head to a big moordgah – a Christmas tree – with its strong branches and lots of leaves providing coverage, climb right to the top and sit up there yarning. We didn't go hungry because we'd make sandwiches or grab a few slices of dampa and dip or butter every morning for our school lunch and take a bottle of kaep as well.

The tree was located in an area known by Nyoongars as Moorni Kaep – the Black Waters – a heavily wooded area. Our hideout was just off the main bush track that nearly all the Nyoongars – Swampies and the Reserve lot alike – took to get to town. Hidden by the thick clumps of greenery, we would listen in on what was being said as people below us made their way past. Nobody ever knew we were there and from our high vantage point we saw an awful lot of goings on, including men and women sneaking around with other people's partners.

One time we were sitting up the tree when a couple we knew came into view. Both were married to other people. They stopped about ten yards from us near an old kwel. They were so close to us we dared not even breathe too loudly. They started kissing passionately, she pressing herself right up close to him. He looked like he was lapping it up. Smiling wicked. Then he put his hand up her skirt. She backed away from him. It was clear the bloke wanted to do more than kiss but the woman told him her husband was waiting for her.

Much to his disappointment, she turned abruptly and walked quickly away. Confused, he was left standing there watching her rush away. No more smiling. That was replaced by some choice swear words.

Next minute, after checking no one could see him, he unzipped his fly. Margie and I looked at each other and put our hands in our mouth to stop from laughing. We thought he was going for a pee. Nothing doing. He pulled his doodle out alright, but then started wanking himself. Right there. He kept checking the path to see if anyone was coming from either direction. He never once looked our way and after a few minutes of working on himself he gave a muffled groan and leaned against the kwel, as if exhausted. Our eyes were big as saucers by what we had seen. If anyone saw us at that time, we could have been mistaken for two big-eyed moke-pokes hidden up that tree. Up until that point we had thought sex was always between two people. That day we hit a real steep learning curve in sex education. This was one bloke who obviously didn't need anyone but himself.

Still shocked, but not daring to giggle about what we had witnessed, we watched him quickly straighten his clothes up and move away as some other people headed down the path. He was a bit older than us and we knew him well. From that day onwards we could never look that bloke straight in the eye. There was always the risk we would tear ourselves laughing in his face. It was wicked. We were wicked for missing school. Wicked for watching such a private act being played out in front of us. But we laughed and laughed for the next week, the following month and from time to time over the following years. When we became adults and knew more about what goes on between a man and a woman, we laughed even more.

Of course, we were found out about ducking school. As was

the rule, we Nyoongars couldn't miss classes without a note from home. I took to writing notes for myself using some illness I read about in my older sister's nurse training manuals.

I also helped write absent notes for Margie when she couldn't think of an illness or good excuse to put down on paper.

One day in our little town where everyone knew everybody else, the school secretary Mrs Johnson said hello to Mum on the street. She said she was sorry to hear about my condition. She offered her help, saying Mum just needed to ask. Curious, Mum asked her, 'What condition are you referring to Mrs Johnson?'

Mum didn't have much time for stickybeaks, especially wadjerlar stickybeaks, but she remained polite.

With a sympathetic look on her face, the secretary replied, 'Lavinia has a type of cancer, doesn't she? That's why she has been away from school for the past three months, right? Oh, Mrs Connell, I am so sorry.'

Being quick on her feet and without answering the questions, Mum said a gracious thank you and let the school secretary know she would get back to her if we needed her help.

Well, the shit really hit the fan then. Mum contacted the school and found out both Margie and I had been truanting on and off for just on three months. To stop any police or Native Welfare involvement, an urgent appointment was made with the headmaster, Mr Clough.

The following Monday morning at nine o'clock sharp, along with Mum and cousin Gertie in their Sunday best, we were seated outside the principal's office. Mum, Gertie, her daughter Margie and me sitting there like four wooden statues. The mood was deadly serious and we realised the possible consequences of what we had done. Nobody was talking. We girls could be taken away and put in a home for wayward girls or even a mission somewhere in the state. All four of us Nyoongar yorgas were at the principal's mercy and, through him, the government's mercy.

Now, Mr Clough was around fifty years old, way over six feet tall and very austere. Straight up and down, it looked like he had a board in his back instead of a spine. This tall, grey-haired man demanded respect. In my mind, he would be right at home commanding soldiers on a military base.

As we sat there contemplating our future, the thick wooden door to his office was opened with a flourish. In my scared frame of mind, he appeared to fill the doorway. Then he invited us in.

He had arranged four chairs together so we were seated in front of his huge, polished wooden desk. He then sat behind his desk facing us. His name – Mr Clough – was printed in bold letters on a name slide sitting front and centre on his desk. In my guilt-ridden mind, the name Clough even rhymed with tough. He didn't waste any time, asking us to give an explanation as to why we had missed so much school. I waited to hear what Margie would say, but she wasn't volunteering anything. So, in a very quiet voice, I offered that I wasn't happy at school. Margie, the big-mouth who told Clem about my crush, just sat there. Never uttered one word.

Anyway, after further discussions and laying down some serious conditions we had to abide by for the rest of the school year, it was agreed that the police would not be involved. Mum, Gertie, Margie and I all breathed a huge sigh of relief.

Mum said, 'Thank you very much, sir. I will be keeping a very close eye on Lavinia from now on.'

He turned to Gertie for her response to the agreement about us not missing any more school. With a quick glance at the name tag on his desk, speaking loudly and very seriously she come out with: 'Yes, Mr Clogg, I'll do the same, Mr Clogg. Thank you very much, Mr Clogg.'

Maybe it was relief at the outcome, but I swore I heard a faint snicker from Mum as she stood up. On the verge of some serious laughter myself at Gertie's mispronunciation, I stood up and looked away. I couldn't look at Mum or Margie. We would have all burst out laughing. With a slight smile on his own face, Mr Clough ushered us out and Mum almost completely lost it in front of him when Gertie said, 'You a good man. Truly a good man. Thank you, Mr Clogg.'

Even before we got outside the corridor, the three of us were doubled up laughing.

Gertie still didn't get it.

When Mum told her how she should say his name, she said, 'Oh my God, no wonder he was smiling at me when we left. But I meant it. That Mr Clogg is a really nice man.'

That killed it again for us. We laughed all the way to the shops.

KYAH SCHOOL

Late in the last term of that year, Margie left school. She was already fourteen and within her rights to do so. I stayed and finished Year 8 but my grades were slightly down. I opted to do a technical course studying the arts, shorthand and typing instead of French and advanced subjects over the next two years. I passed with flying colours. I never ducked another school day. Now it seemed like every Nyoongar person I had grown up with had left. Either they just stopped attending school, had gone away to work or had gone to study in Perth. I had my Irish friends from Fairbridge, but it wasn't the same, and of course we could never see each other or have any fun on weekends.

I still played netball on Saturdays and sometimes went to church on Sunday mornings before helping Mum with all the washing for the week when I got back home. I was growing up. I didn't drink alcohol or smoke, and I kept out of trouble. I would sometimes catch up with my friends Cathy or Benjamin but, like Margie, they had set new directions for themselves. I didn't hate school, but for a long while it was a pretty lonely place for me.

In the last months of my third year in high school, I was sent down to Waroona, a small town about thirty minutes' drive south of Pinjarra, to help my sister Lucy. She had developed some short-term but serious health issues and needed support with caring for her family. Like Pinjarra, it too is sheep and dairy farming country and my uncles and their sons had helped to clear the land for the wadjerlar farmers.

My youngest sister, Hannah, was already living with Lucy, so I wasn't lonely. I was enrolled in Waroona High School and walked the mile to school from her place every day. It was the same distance from our place in Pinjarra to that high school, but in Waroona each morning it was walking uphill all the way – thank goodness I was young and fit – and after school it was all downhill in more ways than one.

I knew a lot of the girls my age who attended Waroona High School because I had competed against them in athletics in primary school and again in netball on the weekends once I started high school. But, apart from being school friends, we never mixed too much. My time was taken up with helping Lucy and going to her Seventh Day Adventist church services in North Yunderup on the weekends. Most times we would pull into Pinjarra on the way back and visit Mum and Dad for an hour or so. At fifteen, I completed my Junior Certificate at Waroona and left high school soon after. I stayed with Lucy and her family until December, then moved back home to Mum and Dad's.

WORKING GIRL

Being back home in Pinjarra with Mum and Dad after staying in Waroona felt really good. There is definitely no place like home. Through the connections of Mum and the other Nyoongar women employed by white families, for a while I managed to go to work in Pinjarra as a babysitter–housemaid for one of the local wadjerlar ladies. She was the wife of the shire president. My first-ever boss had one little boy about three years old, and she had just given birth to a new baby girl. The work was easy and I enjoyed taking care of the two children while their mother recuperated.

Even though I had that job, I still applied for several shop assistant positions in Pinjarra. But each time, I was told the advertised position was not available. Even when the jobs were still advertised as vacant three months later, I was still being told I couldn't get that job. So I stayed at that babysitting–housemaid position for four months, until that family eventually moved away.

When I was almost sixteen, Native Welfare stepped in and got me a job. I was sent to work in Wanneroo, again as a babysitter-housemaid. Mrs Roussell was a white Australian woman married to a Frenchman. I liked working for them and caring for their two young children, though I did wonder why the previous worker had left. It was a beautiful house and Mrs Roussell was a really lovely person. She was a very beautiful woman and a really good boss.

Her parents had a big house in Dalkeith and we visited them

nearly every weekend. I never saw Mr Roussell very much at all. He would take off every morning before daybreak to work on their farm down the road. He would get back very late so it was mainly Mrs Roussell, the little ones and me in the house.

Everything was great for about six months. I would help Mrs Roussell get the kids ready after they had eaten breakfast. Following their bath, I dressed them in day clothes then took them out to play in the yard while she did some cleaning up of her own or all the paperwork for her household.

Whenever the kids took a nap, I would hang the washing out and do whatever else was needed to be done around the house. This included cutting wood and making a fire in the pot belly stove so we all could have a hot shower. We had to turn on a huge generator to get electricity to the house, and we did that every evening from around five o'clock. This was so the little ones could watch cartoons on television and I could do the ironing and use whatever other appliances needing electricity.

Every second evening, Mrs Roussell would do some washing that I would hang out the next morning. This routine was fine. If I wanted to read after the generator was turned off, I used a trusty big torch that Mum and Dad had bought for me, along with a small transistor radio, as a birthday present when I turned fourteen. Most times, though, I was asleep before the generator was switched off. I was working and earning my own money and even managing to save a few dollars as well.

One Saturday morning around 7.30, I got up as usual to help prepare breakfast for the kids and myself. Suddenly Mr Roussell walked into the kitchen. He was stark naked! He was looking straight at me. He knew what he was doing, the nasty bastard. Parading around naked in front of me.

I knew it was his home. I knew he should be able to walk around however he wanted to. But there is a thing called respect. He had none. Not for himself or for his lovely wife. And definitely none for me. I was shocked and embarrassed seeing him walk around with his balls dangling, his penis sticking straight out. I also knew because of the Native Welfare Act and its policies, the balance of power was with him, the white person. Well, this young black girl was having none of that, government policy or not.

I didn't stay to get any breakfast. I turned around and took straight off back to my room and locked my door. For good measure I pushed my bed against it. I was bloody shaken up properly. Mum had warned me about how wadjerlar men could be. She had told me about the white men on the farms and stations where she had worked as a young woman. Horrible white men who treated respectable black women like whores.

Memories of that night when Rhona was beaten and raped by the sergeant came flooding back. I started to shake with fear but I didn't panic. I promised myself that what had been done to Rhona by a white man was not going to be done to me. There was no way I was going to be raped and fall pregnant to a wadjerlar and sent away as punishment for what he had done.

Even though it was broad daylight, I got my big metal torch out of my bag. I was more than prepared and determined to use it as a weapon if that naked arsehole tried to come through my door.

I didn't come out of my room until Mrs Roussell called out for me to help get the kids ready. Thank God her poxy husband had apparently left for work. I was still shaken up. What should I do? Back home in Pinjarra nobody had phones, so I couldn't call anyone. But I knew I had to leave that place. Fuck the money and everything else good about the job. That horrible bare-arsed man had spoiled it for me.

When Mrs Roussell drove us into Dalkeith for our usual weekend visit to her parents' home, after saying hello to them and settling the children in their playroom, with a quick good-bye I caught a bus into the city. I booked a ticket on the *Australind* and caught the train to Pinjarra and walked home to Mum and Dad.

I never went back to that job. I didn't worry about my pay or the few things I had left in Wanneroo at their house. That man was a definite danger to me.

CITY YORGA

A week later, two Native Welfare officers, a man and a woman, came down to talk to us about me not returning to work for Mrs Roussell. She was worried about me. Native Welfare were also concerned and wanted to know what was going on. Mum gave those two officers both barrels. She was so angry. She told them that if they were so worried about me leaving that job, then maybe they should go and work with Mrs Roussell themselves. Her husband could walk around naked in front of them. The female officer's face went crimson when my mum said that.

It was the first time I had ever seen or heard of it, but they ended up apologising to both me and Mum. Those two Native Welfare officers did eventually manage to get the pay due to me, as well as my belongings from Mrs Roussell's house. I really was sorry to have left her and the two kids, and for a while I missed them. But I had to look after myself and I didn't trust that wadjerlar mongrel not to try anything.

I stayed at home for a couple of months helping Mum around the old place. Things were much more basic than at the Roussells' place. I went back to carting the water from the well and doing the washing by hand. But it didn't bother me. I wasn't earning any money, but Dad was still working so I never wanted for anything. Then we heard again from Native Welfare. The letter to Mum said they had organised for me to start a job right in Perth at a florist shop working for the female owner. I would stay in a hostel for young Aboriginal people in Applecross and be supervised by an older couple named Mr and Mrs Grander. They let Mum know this couple had been thoroughly checked out by Native Welfare officers. Two weeks later, I was on my way to live in the hostel.

Every day I caught a bus into the city which dropped me just outside the door of the florist shop in St Georges Terrace. The work was very interesting and I learned quite a bit about how to run a business from Mrs Johnson. Ordering, purchasing, preparing and selling flowers was a challenging and colourful job.

I learned the names of every flower we ordered and how to record every sale with date, time and amount listed in the sales book before signing off.

As well as all that paperwork, I also had to make tea for my boss. She was very, very fussy about that process. I was instructed to boil the water first. Once that was hot, I had to pour a small amount into the teapot to preheat it. I had to swirl the hot water around before emptying that water out. I then put two tablespoons of tea leaves into the now warm pot and filled it with boiling hot water. Finally a knitted tea-cosy was placed over the whole pot to keep its contents hot while it settled for three full minutes or more to 'draw'. Once drawn, it was gently poured into a very dainty pre-warmed cup. Two teaspoons full of sugar came next and lastly, no more than four teaspoons of fresh milk. I had to follow this process for each morning and afternoon tea. I learned fast and never had to do it twice. Ever.

In the back of my mind, I really thought she was a bit kaartwarra, being so fussy about a cuppa. At our place, when anyone made tea, it was a matter of placing a billy can of water on the stove or open fire. As soon the water boiled, a handful of tea leaves was thrown in. The billy can was taken off the heat and set aside for a few minutes. The tea was then poured straight into big mugs to be sweetened. Sometimes, if we had any, bottled, sweetened milk in a can or powered milk was added. But most times at home, our tea was just plain, black and sweet.

Life was pretty good at the hostel. I had my own room and use of most things in the building, although there were some fairly strict rules that applied to everyone. The main one was we had to have quick showers because there were about six of us young people there, plus the two Granders. It was a really mixed bunch living there, with about four Aboriginal people and two white kids from up north. Everyone had somewhere to go each weekday, either to high school, university or work.

After I got there, for the first few weekends on Saturday afternoon, we all went out together for rides to different places in a small bus driven by Mr Grander. But on Sunday morning, everyone was expected to attend church. Sunday afternoon was set aside for studying, reading or letter writing. Television was only allowed to be switched on for the news and a few early evening shows. It was turned off every weeknight at 7.30 sharp.

I was there for a few months before the Granders agreed that it was okay for me to go home to Pinjarra for the weekends. On those weekends, after catching up with Mum and Dad and my family, I spent time with my friend Leira. We were both nearly sixteen at the time, and her breaks from Perth College, an all-girl private school in Mount Lawley where she was completing Year 11, often coincided with my time off from the hostel. Leira and I chose not to meet up in Perth because we were only fifteen and not keen to be wandering around the streets up there. We preferred to be home in Pinjarra.

It seemed to happen gradually but Jason, Leira's older brother, started asking if his sister wanted to join him when he went for a ride somewhere. Of course, I was included in the invitation. On those occasions I took the back seat. Sometimes Benjamin would come too and Jason would insist on Leira sitting in the back with me.

We would drive around in his car and go to the beach in Mandurah or up to see their relatives in East Perth. These were only short visits and we would always be back in Pinjarra before nightfall. That was the only condition Mum and Dad had insisted on whenever I asked if I could go with Leira and her mob. Sometimes we went to the drive-in movies, but her mum and young brother Tedo would always come too.

It was about a month before I turned sixteen that Jason asked my parents if I could go alone to the movies with him. Leira couldn't get every weekend off, so there were times when I was home from the hostel and she was still at college. Anyway, Jason got up enough courage himself to ask Mum and Dad if it was okay, and after some discussion and laying down some ground rules, they gave him the nod.

They knew I was a pretty level-headed young person. My brother Clem came along on those first dates too, so that also put their minds at ease. However, that only worked out for a few weekends with Clem tagging along with us two. Being a young bloke himself, he had his own affairs to worry about. Soon, it was just me and Jason on our own every weekend that I got off from the hostel.

Jason was really good-looking, single, a non-boozer, hardworking with a steady job and he had his own car. In our little town he was considered a catch. He was about four years older than me and still lived at home. From what I knew, he was close to his mother and sisters and cared for the women in his family. I couldn't really fathom what he saw in me. I didn't consider myself that pretty at all. And I definitely wasn't one would call 'worldly'. 'Small town chick' was nearer the mark.

Jason looked after me, and every time he picked me up, he made sure my parents or sisters or someone in my family knew where we were going. From what I could see, he never had trouble getting a girlfriend. So I was a bit surprised and somewhat flattered by Jason's sudden interest in me.

Leira and I were best friends and had been hanging around together since primary school, so Jason wasn't a stranger to me by any means, and he and his family had seen me grow up. My dad worked with his dad. Our mothers played cards together a couple of times a week. Mum and Dad were godparents to Leira, and her parents, Edna and old Tedo, were godparents to my brother Clem. Jason was also good friends with Clem and my cousin Claude. They all played footy in the same team along with other young Nyoongar blokes in town.

I guessed he wanted to be with me because he knew I had a good reputation. A lot of other Nyoongar girls around my age were all sleeping around with different blokes, and in a small town like ours everybody knew about it. Having strict parents and four older brothers, my social movements were closely monitored.

Not that I needed them to be. Even at an early age I set my own moral standards. I'd seen enough drunken shit happen in my young life. I didn't hang around places where everyone was boozing and carrying on. I had no interest in that at all. Like me, my friends didn't drink or smoke and we spent our time playing sport, going to movies, watching *Bandstand* on TV when we could and keeping out of trouble.

KARNYAH

So at sixteen I was a decent young woman and independent now that I was working. In our Nyoongar community it seemed a natural, inevitable progression that Jason and I would get together. But, as it turned out, not everyone in my family was happy about it. Jono and Clem seemed okay with us two keeping company, but for some unknown reason, Trevor and Edwin questioned my being allowed to go out with Jason. They never gave me a reason why they didn't like him. Maybe it was because he didn't drink alcohol and didn't mix too much with them. Or maybe because he kept mainly to himself. I often heard them call him an arrogant prick.

But they never said much when sober. As soon as they got drunk they argued with Mum and Dad and called me some real filthy names in the bargain. Forget tomboy nicknames like Lumberjack and Luigi. It was now 'slut', 'bitch' and 'moll'. It was totally unwarranted and it hurt me deeply. When I knew they were getting on the kgaepa, I took off and kept right out of their way until I knew they would be sober.

Clem, my youngest brother, who when I was in high school, had threatened to punch my first crush's head in, told our drunken brothers to mind their own business. He rightly pointed out that I was their sister, not their daughter. He always defended Mum, Dad and me whenever those other two started up. They got so bad, Clem even called them out for fight a few times. He also dared them to go to Jason and repeat what they were saying. Tell it straight to his face. Not pick on me and the oldies. They must have been scared of a confrontation with Jason though because they stuck to their cowardly ways, swearing at me and stressing out our parents.

I remember quite clearly there was one time I was ordered by the police to go down to the police station. I found out from the police that Trevor wanted Jason to be arrested and charged with carnal knowledge of a girl under sixteen. Talk about karnyah. It was a huge embarrassment and humiliation for me.

I was questioned by the munartj about the intimate details of what we did. Also, where we had gone, and with whom. However, at that stage nothing sexual had happened between us. We were always in the company of his family or mine. Also, thank God, I had respect for myself and my body. I also knew about the law.

As expected, the police didn't believe me so I was taken up to the hospital and examined by the doctor. I was given the all clear. Mum was so angry with what Trevor had done. She told him to get his own kids and worry about them not me. I was her and Dad's daughter, not his.

I was so glad that Mum had stuck up for me, but the shame of it all was humiliating. Having those white men asking me personal questions about my body and about sex, and smirking all the time. I had no option but to answer them because they had the power over me. The Native Welfare still had the right to put me in a home for wayward girls if I didn't. The only good thing about the whole incident was the sergeant who had attacked and raped Rhona was not stationed there anymore. Thank God. He had been transferred away a few years before. I knew Jason had been taken to the police station and questioned at length too, though he didn't talk to me very much about what happened to him. But I did sense he was very angry.

In some ways, that incident moved my relationship with Jason to a new, closer level. We became partners in persecution. I was glad to go back to work in Perth and on the weekends I spent less and less time at home if Trevor and Edwin were there. I would go see my parents, then head out to catch up with Jason and Leira.

Around this time, my brother Clem decided to join the army as a volunteer. It was 1966 and the war in Vietnam had already started. Mum and Dad weren't at all happy about him enlisting. As an Aboriginal man, he could easily be exempt with no penalty. But he did all the tests and was accepted into the Australian Infantry. My main backstop had gone off to train to fight for his country.

I often thought about my other two brothers Trevor and Edwin too. The ones I used to know. Those two who had cared about me when I was growing up. I wondered where the hell they had vanished to. They appeared to have been replaced by two idiots who swore at me every time they got drunk.

I was so glad when Edwin got conscripted and went to the Eastern States for his army training in the Royal Australian Engineers, and Trevor moved away to live down south with his new wife and her family. It made my life so much easier whenever I was there with Mum and Dad. Unfortunately, Trevor didn't stay away too long.

BOODJARI YORGA

I was still travelling home to Pinjarra every weekend and heading back on the train to the hostel in Applecross on Sunday evenings. It was a few months after I turned sixteen that I woke up feeling sick one Friday morning. I suspected I might be pregnant because Jason and I had crossed that legal line two weeks after my birthday. I didn't tell anyone anything until I got back home. I wasn't a dummy. My sisters before me had all had morning sickness. So, the first thing I did was tell Mum about it. She wasn't shocked or angry and organised a doctor's appointment. Sure enough, I was boodjari. Sixteen years old and going to be a mum. Actually, I was much older than some of the girls in town who at sixteen already had one or two children. It wasn't unusual for Nyoongar girls to have babies when they were as young as twelve and thirteen. Back then, in our Nyoongar community at least, sixteen was seen as a respectable age to have your first baby.

I do believe it shocked some of my siblings when I got pregnant so young. In some ways, life got a whole lot harder for me after it became known that I was expecting a baby. Truth be told, except for Mum, Dad and a few others, my family more or less wiped their hands of me when I got pregnant.

This being my first baby, I wanted to spend more time with Mum. My body was changing and although I was still physically strong, my emotions were a rollercoaster. So I stayed at home with my parents, getting advice and care from them. Jason was working out bush with my cousins.

But it wasn't easy because I wasn't the only person living at home. A few of my brothers and sisters and their partners were there too. In our Nyoongar community, it wasn't unusual for family members to return to their parents' place if they couldn't find work elsewhere. They brought their small families with them.

It led to overcrowding, but in keeping with government policies of the time, all Nyoongars had to have a permanent address or they could be charged with vagrancy. If that happened, they could be jailed and their kids could be taken from them.

Mum and Dad never turned any of their children away and somehow made room for all of us. As a large family living in a small home, we managed to get along most of the time. But things would change when some members of the family started drinking alcohol. I clearly recall being sworn at really dirty by some of my drunken siblings. The swearing and name-calling I had experienced before got worse now that I was boodjari. Every time it happened, I was in tears, which wasn't good for me or my baby. I felt threatened by their words so I would take off to Uncle Levi and Aunty May's place until they sobered up. I knew I had to protect myself.

It came to a head one night as we were quietly strolling back from their place. Mum and I overheard my sister Rita, my brother Trevor, and his wife, Mary, talking loudly about me. They were drunk. They were saying that they would abort my baby or 'boot it out of me'. Either way, they didn't think it was right that I carry Jason Kagan's kid. There was no thought about the fact that my baby belonged to me as well. That it was their niece or nephew I was carrying. I got the impression that me being pregnant and unwed at sixteen was not the issue. For some reason unknown to me they didn't like Jason at all.

With real fear in her voice and talking just above a whisper, Mum told me to run to Aunty Ruby's place and stay there until something was sorted out. So in the middle of that very dark night I found myself walking, and at times almost running, along the bush back track to Aunty Ruby's.

Unlike at the old reserve, Aunty Ruby's new place was nearly a mile south of our place. The government had built new iron-and-tin houses with running water and electricity included for all the reserve residents. But they had moved them further away from where we lived.

I had never felt so alone. I was upset and crying and so scared. It was Pinjarra after all, and that place has so many ghost stories I dreaded going by myself so late in the pitch black. But the alternative was worse.

And so I ran through the night to save my unborn baby. I was never as glad as when I finally saw the lights of Aunty Ruby's house.

Their actions meant I could no longer stay with Mum and Dad. After all, I was a single person. My sister and brother had their children living at Mum and Dad's place with them. If they were kicked out by my parents, they faced vagrancy charges and the children faced being removed and put in missions. So, the next day agreements were struck and arrangements were made between my parents and Jason's, and I moved in with Jason and his family at Hilton Road on the Nyoongar reserve.

In some ways, the transition from being single to being in a live-in relationship with Jason was relatively easy. Over the years, through my friendship with Leira, I had already spent a lot of time with the family. I knew how they operated and what would be expected of me. However, it was different and permanent now. Not like before, when I would be just visiting. Also, being several months pregnant, I was about to become a big part of Jason's life. His responsibility.

I do believe that to most of my in-laws, I was an unwanted burden. Of course I was carrying their oldest son's child, their grandchild, and that was the only reason I was allowed to live with them. In typical Nyoongar fashion, some of them let me know in no uncertain terms how they felt. More so after they'd had a few drinks.

It seems my brothers and sister weren't the only ones who needed kgaepa to give voice to what they felt inside. Yet, even when they were sober, with some of my in-laws there was always the negative comments aimed at or about me.

Jason himself never said anything bad to me, but I sensed he was not totally happy with the situation. After all, he was twenty-one, had a good job and his own car. Settling down with a young, somewhat naive, woman and a baby was not on his agenda. There were persistent rumours that he was already the father of a baby girl to one of my cousins. And he hadn't stayed with her at all while she was pregnant. Their relationship was over way before my time, so I wasn't too fussed about it. Jason always denied that the baby was his so it wasn't an issue between us.

Despite all that, us two got on okay, but he had to go where the work was, so he was away quite a bit. I heard all the snarky comments from some of his family but put up with them. Now that it was unsafe to be at my home with Mum and Dad, what choice did I have?

If it was up to Native Welfare, I would be put in a home for unwed mothers and my baby given up for adoption to white people. Although it was in the mid-1960s, we Nyoongars were still ruled strictly by the government. It wasn't until my beautiful baby boy was born five months later that my baby's dad finally told his family never to run me down again or they would have to deal with him. I think Jason was waiting to see if my baby was actually his. I don't know why he had any doubts about that because I had never been with anyone but him.

FIRST NINNI ONE

It was a Saturday morning in March when my water broke. Prior to that, with Trevor and Mary still down south, I had been spending a few days with Mum and Dad while I waited for my baby. Also, Jason was still away working out bush with my cousins and wouldn't be back for nearly a week. My son was born just about the date my doctor predicted. With a mass of curly black hair and a cute little chubby face, he weighed in at eight pounds six ounces. He came into this world with a fair bit of drama though.

The afternoon before I started getting labour pains, Clem had come home on leave from the army and overnight there had been some happy celebrations taking place. He had brought with him his white mate, Troy, who was in the same army unit. They'd brought along a few beers and Mum had cooked a lovely big meal for her youngest son. After the feed, everyone sat around the fire catching up with their yarns. Mum and I settled down early, but Dad and the blokes sat up until late yarning and drinking beer.

The next day, Dad (who was still a bit hungover), Mum and I got up early and made breakfast. We were sitting around the fire having a cuppa when I felt a 'pop' in my lower belly. Next minute, clear fluid started flowing down my legs. Feeling a bit alarmed, I turned to Mum and Dad and told them what had happened.

Dad said, 'Must be her time, Mum.'

He then cleared out of the room, closing the door behind him. Mum got up and helped me get changed into dry clothes.

Next minute, I felt a cramp-like pain and doubled over, holding my belly. Well, that's when the panic began. Mum, who had given birth to all her own babies in a hospital, started yelling at Dad to do something.

My Dad – the father of ten who had not witnessed any of his children being born – came back into the room and tried to calm Mum down. She promptly stepped towards him and punched him on the chest.

'This is her first baby, old boy! We don't know what is going to happen. There could be complications. You wanna deliver baby here? Get help for our daughter now, you old grey-haired bastard!'

Mum went to hit him again. Dad backed out the door and took off to the shed where the two soldiers had fallen asleep on beds they had made on the floor. He rallied them up to go and get an ambulance, a taxi and even the police. Get somebody! Anybody! We needed help. Still half-cut, they both got up and came to see what was happening in the house.

When Dad, Clem and Troy came through the front door into the kitchen, Mum immediately started shouting at Dad again to do something. After checking with me that I was okay for now, those two blokes took off running. Still in full uniform with heavy army boots on and suffering from bad hangovers, they ran the mile to town and came back home in the taxi in record time. The Murray District Hospital in Pinjarra was situated along the South Western Highway. It too is about a mile to the east from our place. Mum and Dad came with me in the taxi, and Mum was definitely relieved to be on our way.

Once Matron Daniel had me settled in the maternity ward, my parents left me with promises of coming back later on during visiting hours. Jason's mum and Leira came in to see me too. They stayed for about fifteen minutes, promising to get word to Jason that I was in hospital and ready to have our baby.

Throughout the day, my pains got progressively stronger until about eight o'clock in the evening, when I was moved into the birth preparation room. It was right next door to the baby delivery room. I could hear that there was already another woman in there. She was crying softly and praying, but every couple of minutes she would call out in pain.

Now, back in the day, there was no electronic button you could press to bring nursing staff. There was only a big brass, hand-held school bell that patients rang to get the nurses' attention. The labour ward itself was some distance away from both the nursing station and the general maternity wards. It was down the long corridor and around the corner. It was also soundproof.

By this time, my pains were getting very strong and happening far more regularly. My contractions were down to about five minutes apart and I could hear the woman already in the baby delivery room getting louder and louder. She was crying, praying and shouting in Italian now. It sounded like she was going to deliver her baby on her own. She was in real pain and desperately needed help. As frequent as my own contractions were, I knew I had to do something to help her.

So in between my own labour pains, which were coming stronger and more frequently, I rolled off my preparation room bed. Once standing, I made my way to her room and pushed open the door. She looked my way, tears streaming down her young tortured face, fear and agony combined. Her eyes were pleading for help. I estimated her baby was due any minute.

I felt really scared for her and her baby. So, with one hand holding my own big belly and the other holding onto the wall, I forced my way back to the preparation room and grabbed that ugly old school bell. With one mighty swing, I pulled open the massive door leading to the corridor. Pain doubled me over.

I thank God I was young and strong. I took a deep breath and let that one big contraction pass. Then I rang that bell for all I was worth, still leaning on the heavy door for support. The ringing echoed so loudly down that empty hospital corridor I reckon they heard it outside in the gardens.

I was never so glad to hear Matron's heavy footsteps, practically running down the corridor towards the labour ward. She was followed by the two other nurses on duty. Matron and the first nurse went straight through to help the other woman while the second nurse took the still-ringing bell from my hand and helped me back into the prep room, just as another huge pain hit me. I grabbed my belly as I doubled over again.

Once my pain passed, I managed to climb back onto my bed with help from the nurse. Relief flooded through me. At least that other mother had help now. It must have been less than three minutes later when I heard one wicked deafening scream, then a baby crying. At least she had delivered her bub safely, thank God.

I still had half an hour or so of labour pains before my doctor came and helped deliver my baby boy. Doctor Bain was dressed in a tuxedo because he had come directly from the local golf club trophy presentation. He looked real dapper, but with all the pain I was in it wouldn't have mattered if he was dressed in a tracksuit. Still, he had managed my pregnancy all the way through and I was relieved to have him there to help me deliver my firstborn.

At times, the pain was almost unbearable. I clung to the gas mask every chance I got. It helped me cope, but I remember hallucinating – seeing different family members talking to me, even though there was only the doctor, Matron and the nurses in the delivery ward with me.

Finally, nearly eighteen hours after I left Mum and Dad's home, my baby arrived safe and sound and so, so beautiful. All the pain of those last few hours disappeared when they placed my baby boy on my chest. I felt instant love for him. I remember Doctor Bain telling me I had done really well. That was the last thing I heard. Utter relief from all the strain and stress of the past few hours hit me like a sledge hammer and I fell sound asleep knowing my baby was safe, healthy and in good hands.

It was during visiting hours on the second day that Matron came into my shared room with two bunches of flowers. She set them up in vases and put them on my locker. She told me they were from the family of the young Italian woman I had helped when I was in the prep room. Later, I also received boxes of chocolates and a huge box of fruit from them. She too had a healthy baby boy with masses of dark curly hair, just like my son.

TYING THE KNOT

My beautiful first son was named Jason Clem Connell. As was the law back then, children of unmarried mothers could only take their mother's surname. So he carried mine. Our son carrying the Connell name wasn't an issue for me and Jason because we were happy together and our baby boy was healthy. Getting married wasn't really a priority for us either. But to put it right in the eyes of the law and our Nyoongar community, and at the insistence of the oldies, seven months after baby Jason was born his father and I were married. My son and I became Kagans too.

Since I was only seventeen years old, my dad and mum had to give written consent for me to get married. I would have had to be twenty-one to sign for myself. But they did this with a good heart, and once written permission was given, with a lot of help from Mum, Jason's mum, Lucy and Leira, we went ahead and made plans for Jason and I to tie the knot.

At the time we were still living with his family. It was pretty crowded at Hilton Road because there were only three small bedrooms, plus a combined kitchen and dining area and lounge room space. It had a stove, a kitchen sink over built-in cupboards, a dining table and chairs and two lounge chairs – effectively only one room for the living and eating area. There was also a small laundry off to one side which had one concrete trough and a tiny shower cubicle. To access the toilet we had to walk outside, turn a sharp left, then through a door attached to the house. There was also a front verandah running the length of the house front. One good thing was that the house had power and water laid on. In all, there were nine people living in that small galvanised iron and corrugated tin house. Jason's parents and younger brother Tedo; Jason, baby Jason and me; Jason's sister Patty, her bloke, Marty, and their son Berny. On the weekends when Leira came back, she slept on the long lounge chair.

I had no income because social security payments from the government had not been introduced yet. Jason paid his mum board money for us three. What he gave to me was my only income, except for what my mum gave me whenever she had a couple of dollars to spare.

Sometime after I had my son, I did get a one-off bonus from the government and that lump sum came in handy. Of course it didn't last long and was used to buy clothes for baby Jason, a couple of personal items for me and food for the whole family. The government also gave all Australian mothers – young ones and older ones – of children under sixteen an endowment every fortnight. So it was good to get a few dollars of my own on a regular basis.

That bit of boya meant I was able to chuck in my share along with everyone else to pay for the cost of getting married. The local Anglican church didn't charge anything. Maybe it was because Leira, Cathy and I had been confirmed in that church a few years earlier and we had been pretty regular churchgoers since then. We had to pay the shire for using the youth club hall for the reception, but Dad and Mum had that covered.

Leira and Lucy were my bridesmaids. Jason's brother-in-law Brian and my brother Clem were the best men. Being over twenty-one, both Lucy and Brian could sign the marriage certificate as witnesses.

My wedding dress was very pretty. It was white, knee length and very lacy. It had been given to me by the wife of one of Jason's wadjerlar mates. After my baby was born, my seventeen-year-old figure went straight back, so the small A-line dress fitted me perfectly. I also had a waist-length white lace veil which set off the pretty dress beautifully. Leira and Hannah helped me with braiding and pinning small blue flowers in my long blonde hair. I did my own make-up and thought I actually looked beautiful. This was echoed by Mum, Lucy and Jono when he drove us to the church.

My wedding bouquet, like the flowers for the tables, were picked *from fruit trees in Gordon Road and put together by Lucy, Leira* and me. My previous stint in the florist shop in Perth sure came in handy for the arrangements.

Our actual wedding was anything but a typical 'country' bash. When I entered the packed church, with Dad by my side, everyone started clapping and cheering. The loud noise didn't seem to bother our baby boy who was fast asleep on his Aunty Patty's lap in the front row. And even though I was nervous, I couldn't help but smile. When I saw Jason, I smiled even more. Though he too seemed a bit nervous, he looked so handsome in his wedding suit. He smiled at me and my heart melted. At that moment I knew I had made the right decision. I loved him and wanted to spend the rest of my life with him.

After the ceremony, we moved on to the reception at the local youth club hall. When we had first inspected it a few weeks prior, there didn't seem to be enough light and that made the hall appear pretty dull. The table and chairs were very basic and bare. But it looked a whole lot better once the bridesmaids added colourful tablecloths and the flowers were put in place.

All the food was put on one table and people helped themselves, buffet style. There was an open invitation for all the local Nyoongars to attend. The women were asked to bring a plate each, so there was plenty of food for everyone. In typical small-town style, Mum and Lucy made and decorated my wedding cake themselves. It had only the one layer, but it looked big and beautiful and tasted fantastic.

Many female guests went all out with their pretty dresses. Several even made their own gowns at the sewing club held every Tuesday and Thursday afternoon up near Hilton Road. They looked real flash. All the men in the wedding party scrubbed up really smart too in their white shirts, dark suits and highly polished black shoes. Nearly everything the blokes wore was bought from the local second-hand shop and they looked great.

Because it was the mid-1960s, the women in their colourful dresses, also styled up with bright make-up and even hairspray. Some of them put rouge on their cheeks along with a splash of red on their lips and either blue or green eye shadow. In our small-town Nyoongar community it was unusual to see them so dolled up. But then this was a special occasion.

There was music too, from a patch-up, put-together-on-the-day band initially made up of one drummer and one guitarist. Then my Uncle Mordy turned up with his piano accordion and he really tickled the ivories. They were soon joined by Gertie's husband, Dan, with his silver spoons to knock out a moorditj beat. Finally, there was some music the sober ones could dance to! Before Uncle Mordy came along, only the boozers were rocking. But sparked-up Nyoongars will dance to anything, just as long as there's a good beat.

After a few beers, some fullas got up to sing along with the band. They were so out of tune, sounding like wounded cats, they were soon ushered off the stage. One minor argument started, but that was quickly sorted out and everyone got on with having a good time.

Some long-lost cousins from Moora turned up, and my pregnant niece, Mindy, went into labour for her first baby halfway through the celebrations and was rushed to hospital. In our small community, the wedding and all the funny things that had happened would be the talk of the town for us Nyoongars in the weeks to follow. At the end of the night, our little family unit went back to Jason's parent's home – Jason, Lavinia and baby Jason Clem Kagan.

DARK CLOUDS LOOMING

My life settled into some sort of routine in the months after our marriage. We were still living at my in-laws' place on Hilton Road when one quiet Sunday afternoon a woman came to the door. Her name was Lonny and she had only been in town a few months. Apparently she was connected to me on my dad's side, although I didn't know her at all. When she turned up at the house, the first person she spoke with was Jason's sister Patty.

After a quick nod of acknowledgement to me, Lonny and Patty stepped out onto the front verandah, closing the front door behind them. A couple of stickybeak kids rushed to the nearest louvred window, peeping out and straining their ears to hear what was being said. When Jason's mum told them to get out to the back and play, they took off straight away. Their place at the window was then taken by curious adults.

Next minute, Patty came out to the backyard where we were cooking sausages on the fire for lunch. She asked us if anyone knew where her bloke Marty was. She was about to walk off, but then turned towards me and Jason and said, 'Jason, that woman just said she slept with Marty. And you too. What the fuck is going on, brother? What you and Marty been up to?'

We could see Patty was already angry. Now the tears were starting to flow as well. She was so upset she yelled at everyone there, 'Where the fuck is Marty, the prick? We got to have this out now!' Then with tears streaming down her face, she went out the front door screaming for him.

Deadly serious, I turned to Jason and asked him straight out about what the woman had said to Patty. At first he denied it but I knew – and he knew I knew – he was lying. Guilt was written all over his face.

He came towards me winyarn way, arms outstretched, shaking his head. I was having none of it. I hit him in the face with my fist. He tried to pin my arms, but I twisted out of that and went for him again. I pulled at his hair and landed another punch to his face. I tried to scratch his eyes out, instead leaving two bloody welts *down his cheek*.

Absolutely shocked, he took a few steps back and took off into our room. Before he could shut the door, I followed and picked up the first thing I could grab – the heavy wooden doorstop. I threw it straight at his head. He ducked and it just missed him. He must have seen I was gunna kill him because he came towards me and cracked me with his knuckles right on my forehead. Wrong move! It didn't stop me and I kept going towards him. I looked for something else to throw at him. He pushed me backward onto our bed and took off running out the bedroom door. I stood up and again grabbed the wooden doorstop to hit him, but he had bolted out the front door.

Our quiet Sunday afternoon in the family backyard was now shattered. Somehow Leira and her mum grabbed me and calmed me down. Just a few months after our marriage, here was this woman coming over to tell Patty what had taken place with Marty and Jason!

God knows what Patty said or did to Marty when she caught up with him. I saw him a few days later with a wicked black eye. Normally Patty had the gentlest nature, and this whole business had obviously hurt her deeply for her to give him that black eye. She was a big woman and he was a skinny man. I felt no pity for him at all.

I was told later Jason went to the hospital that evening with a broken wrist and two hairline fractures further up his arm. Apparently, that happened when he had hit me on the forehead. He was in plaster for five weeks. I couldn't care less. I didn't have anything wrong with me. No bruising, no headaches, nothing. Anger and adrenaline can be a dangerous combination.

He stayed right out of my way for four weeks or more. I still lived with his family. My son and I were okay there. His mum, Edna, said it was alright and that I had done nothing wrong. But after cleaning up the house, I spent a good deal of every day at my brother Jono's. Nothing much was said to me about Lonny or what had happened that Sunday. However, my mother-in-law did say that we should try and sort things out for the baby's sake.

It was about three weeks later that I woke up feeling a sick. I was sweating profusely and I had a high temperature. Jason wasn't around, so even though I was feeling dizzy, I packed my baby into his pusher and walked the short distance down the road to Jono's. I told him I was feeling sick, so he said for me to lie down on the couch and he would get me a Bex and make me a cup of tea. I lay down and that's the last I remember.

I woke up in hospital. Not our local one in Pinjarra. I had been picked up and transported by ambulance straight to King Edward Memorial Hospital for Women in Subiaco. The doctors told me I had a bad kidney infection and I was severely dehydrated. They also told me I was eight weeks pregnant and that there was a real danger of losing my unborn baby. I have never prayed so much. I prayed every night for my unborn baby to be alright. I had my own ward and spent most of the days I was in hospital in isolation, totally alone. The staff were friendly enough. I was bedridden for ten days and after pumping medicine into me via a drip and taking a multitude of tablets I was able to walk around. Once I got back on my feet, they kept me in another four days. In all I was fourteen days in hospital.

After being in hospital for two weeks I went back to my in-laws' home. It was so good to see my baby boy. I had missed him so much while I was in hospital but I knew he would have been alright with his Nanna Edna and Aunty Leira. They both loved him so much.

Jason, the mongrel cheat, crawled back. After all, I was boodjari again and we were living with his family in their home. Like his mum said, 'We did it for the baby's sake.' Only now it would be for two babies' sakes.

Life was never the same for me after that. The hurt of his betrayal burrowed deep. I felt sad and angry, and at times a sense of shame, even though I had done nothing wrong. I know I never fully trusted Jason again. And I don't think he trusted how I would react in the future if I got angry with him.

Life moves on. His broken wrist healed and the plaster came off. But there was no medicine to heal my broken heart. I was only seventeen, just married and pregnant again.

I gave thanks to God when I delivered my second son, Aimon, the following August. Just like his brother Jason, he was a beautiful chubby baby with lots of black hair, though he looked more like me. He weighed in at nine pounds two ounces. To me, knowing that he nearly never made it to even being born seemed to make him all the more precious.

In some peculiar way, I felt that this baby was mine. With our first born, being the oldest son of an oldest son, everyone made a real fuss of him, especially my in-laws. They all spoiled him rotten. His aunty and uncle took baby Jason for a ride in their car if he couldn't settle of an evening. His Nanna Edna took great pleasure just being in her grandson's company. With Aimon, I had *my* son. He liked being around me and his dad. There was very little drama around his arrival, except when he was being born, I did need extra help. Doctor Bain had to use forceps to get him out of the birth canal. This resulted in Aimon being born with two little black eyes.

Like his mum and dad, his big brother adored him. Aimon was his baby and he definitely wouldn't let any other kid come near him. He wanted to carry him around, but being only eighteen months old himself, the best Jason Junior got was to sit and nurse his little brother, which he did all the time!

Once Aimon started to crawl, he followed his big brother everywhere. From the start, even though they looked very much alike, everyone could see they had different personalities. However, there was brotherly love between them and their bond was rock solid.

ON THE MOVE

When Aimon was about seven months old, Jason and I were offered a State Housing home in Medina, which is located about forty miles north of Pinjarra. We were granted this on the basis of Jason's reliable income and we readily accepted the offer. Jason, along with several other local Nyoongar men, had found steady work in an abattoir about eight miles south of Fremantle. Every day they travelled the forty-eight miles there and back to Pinjarra, though they car-pooled and shared the cost of fuel. Having a home in Medina would definitely save us money because it brought us much closer to his work.

After paying the deposit and a month's rent in advance, we picked up the keys. To say we were surprised when we saw the place is an understatement. We couldn't believe it. To me, it was like a palace. The place was a double brick and tile home, with thick carpets and blinds and pretty curtains on the windows in the lounge and all three bedrooms. There were tiles on the kitchen, bathroom and laundry floors. A truly serendipitous moment for sure! All our lives we had been living with family in crowded conditions. This house was a far cry from my mum and dad's place and Jason's parents' home on the reserve. Not only was it a beautiful house, it was ours for as long as we wanted.

The big move to Medina happened not too long after the government had held a referendum for us black people to be acknowledged as people and citizens in our own country. Before, in lay terms, we were told we had been classified as fauna and had to apply to the government to be recognised as Australian citizens. The good old Citizenship Rights papers. Our mob still had to prove we were upstanding people who could speak the English language. We had to be free from any diseases and act in a civilised manner at all times. The hardest rule was our lot had to cut all ties from other 'non-recognised' Aboriginal people, family included. Like my mum, I couldn't understand why these government rules existed at all.

For instance, my brothers had been trained in the Australian Army. Just like our uncles who had already fought in previous world conflicts like the Second World War and Korea, Clem and Edwin would have gone to Vietnam to fight. Our lot could go to war for our country and maybe even die for it but, according to the government, as Aboriginals they were not considered to be Australian citizens. Although we wouldn't dare say it in public, a lot of us Nyoongars thought it was really stupid. Holding Citizenship Rights papers was like having a passport to move around in our own country when our ancestors have lived here forever.

Although not very interested in politics, us Nyoongars were told that the success of the 1967 referendum meant we would be allowed to vote in federal and state elections. The majority of Australian voters were all for it. Although it wasn't compulsory for Aboriginal people to vote, many of our lot enrolled to do so anyway. Before this time, no Nyoongar I knew, including my parents got to vote. It would not become compulsory for Aboriginal people until 1984.

Now, in theory at least, with the referendum of 1967 we had some of the same rights as everyone else in our country. Now we were counted as people and, if we wanted to, we could go and drink kgaepa in the pubs. Some Nyoongars welcomed the decision to be able to do that, but it also created problems. The government may have given us the okay to vote, and in some ways we could be seen as equals to white people, but not everyone liked the outcome. Prejudices still existed and it took a long time for acceptance.

Also, it meant that now alcohol was easily accessible to our mob and for some people that was like a red flag to a bull. For some Nyoongar families, hard times became harder. Jason and I didn't drink alcohol, so at the time it didn't impact on our lives too much. However, through his work, Jason made friends with some wadjerlar blokes and he joined their local darts team. Competitions were held in the local pub and he began spending a lot of time there with his new mates.

Our little family settled into our new address. It was there that Aimon shocked the hell out of Jason Junior. He was used to Aimon crawling after him everywhere he went. So when the little brother actually stood up and walked towards him, arms outstretched, Jason started screaming, ran to me and hid behind my skirt. Aimon was walking straight towards us, taking his first baby steps towards his big gnoony. I had to sit on a chair, pick Jason up and cuddle him. Aimon was only seven months old and walking, and that surprised everyone.

The years in Medina were another period of growing up for me as well. I stayed at home, looking after our two boys, while their dad went to work. Jason finished up at the abattoir and got a job working for the nearby Kwinana Shire Council. Things were not too bad. Again he made friends with his workmates and we settled into a routine to make a home for the four of us.

On some weekends we would head down to Pinjarra and stay with Jason's family. Each time, I took Jason Junior and Aimon to see my mum and dad as well so they would know their mob on my side. Other times, family would come up and stay with us in Medina. When that happened, I was glad for the company.

It was also around this time that we realised our home was

haunted. Since I was a little girl I have had this inner voice that has been guiding me but I didn't say too much about it to anyone. Yet from the day we moved in my inner voice kept telling me there was another invisible presence in the house. I tried to ignore it but things would happen that we could not explain. Jason Junior started talking to people who weren't there and Aimon didn't wander too far from my side.

On separate occasions, both my mum and mother-in-law told us about seeing the spirit of a woman when they came to help out with the housework and look after their grandsons. It got so I didn't like being in that house alone with the kids.

It added to my sense of isolation. I was happy to go to Pinjarra on the weekends. At least down there I could get a peaceful night's sleep.

Then Jason started drinking kgaepa. He was twenty-five. I do believe it was due to his friends at darts and the ease with which he could now get alcohol. Once he started drinking booze, he would spend Thursday, Friday and Saturday evenings at the pub and come home only after it was closed. He still worked hard, paid the bills and put food on the table, but I found it difficult to raise two boys more or less by myself, especially as I was boodjari again.

Aimon was going on two years old by then and, because I was pregnant again, I was having a hard time coping with my growing boys. Both my mum and Jason's mum often stayed with us a number of different times to help out with the housework and to look after their grandsons.

BABY GIRL

Our beautiful ninni yorga was born early in July, about sixteen months after we moved to Medina. I had booked into the local hospital, which was straight across the road from our house. The pregnancy was going well apart from morning sickness at the beginning and the unusual craving to eat chocolate, pickled onions, hot chips and ice cream all at the same time. However, about a month before I was due, a boil developed on my left leg and my doctor ordered me to go to King Edward Memorial Hospital up in Perth. They took all sorts of tests and I was given strong antibiotics and some painkillers. I was sent back home and told to rest. That proved difficult with two active toddlers.

What happened next changed everything. About ten days later a huge multi-headed carbuncle came up on my left knee. It hurt so much it made me piss. I couldn't walk properly and carrying the extra weight from pregnancy made it excruciatingly painful. Again I was sent to King Edward, and this time they booked me to stay in hospital. I was put on an intravenous drip and I was given antibiotic injections and strong painkillers every four hours to protect me and my unborn baby. As the antibiotics started kicking in, the nurses would try and squeeze the boil to get the pus out. The pain I felt when they squeezed it made me cry. I could hardly stand, but I made myself walk to the toilet so I didn't have to sit on a bedpan. That was adding insult to injury!

My hormones were also playing havoc with me. I was in pain and tears came easily every time the nurses had to treat my leg. I was missing my two sons and crying for them as well. Their dad had taken both boys to Pinjarra to stay with his family, so I knew they would be cared for. But I wanted to see them. Jason was still going to work during the week and told me he would head to Pinjarra on Friday after darts to look after the two boys. No time to come and visit me in hospital. He did ring a few times though. Just to leave messages with staff. Back then, patients didn't have a bedside phone so he could not talk directly with me.

I was in hospital for twelve days before the carbuncle came to a huge, ugly, pussy head. Two Catholic nuns who had just graduated from nursing were part of the nursing team. I don't know what they thought when I started swearing in Nyoongar whenever they treated my knee. But they were very good and spoke kindly to me. I could see it pained them each time they had to give me a needle. Finally they squeezed all the pus out of it. It left a big dent in my leg, but I felt so much relief to have that bloody thing cleared up. I was sick of all the antibiotic injections which stung like hell every time they gave me one.

By this time, the specialist had talked with me about bringing my baby on. He wanted to induce me because my due date was less than two weeks away. Previously Aboriginal women had no say if and when they wanted to be induced. Times had changed but really, I was in no position to argue. My unborn baby was in good health, so I agreed. Plus, I wanted to get out of that hospital and back to my two boys.

So the induction was organised for the following morning. With that decided, I rang and left a message with the local police sergeant to pass the details of the scheduled delivery on to Jason. They induced me early the next morning. It wasn't long before the familiar pains started and I went into labour a few hours later.

My beautiful baby girl was born that night, weighing in at ten pounds two ounces – heavier than both her big brothers. She had long blonde ringlets and the sweetest little chubby face. When she opened her eyes, they were the prettiest colour I had ever seen. She was so beautiful, I was certain God had sent me an angel.

At first, her eyes were green like her Nanna Edna's, then they seemed to turn blue when I put blue clothes on her. Some years earlier, I had seen a coloured photo of my Irish grandfather, my dad's father. My baby girl had the same blue eyes as the man in that photo. Her great-grandfather.

I was over the moon because at last I had my baby girl. She was born the same week Stevie Wonder's song 'For Once in My Life' was playing on the radio. Those words meant so much to me. Here was a girl child that would stick by me for life. Us two yorgas together forever. The pain of the carbuncle, me not being able to walk, the struggle of being in labour and being away from family all faded. I had my girl and she was absolutely beautiful. I thanked God over and over for giving this precious little life to me.

And she took to breastfeeding straight away. It was while I was giving my baby her first feed and touching her little head that I noticed a lump behind her ear. Panic gripped me. I switched on the bed lamp for a better look. In the bright light I could see that it was a small boil that looked ready to burst. I felt it again and suddenly pus started oozing out. Trying not to panic, I grabbed some tissues and wiped it away. Then I rang the bell for the nurse.

By the time the nurse got there nearly all the pus had seeped out. All that remained was a clean wound behind her little ear. The nurse said the boil on my baby's head must have been caused by the carbuncle that I had had on my knee. She cleaned the wound with antiseptic. Later, she came back and gave me an additional antibiotic injection. Through all my fear for her wellbeing, my little angel didn't even cry once.

The next morning, after a good night's sleep, I rang the police sergeant in Pinjarra to tell him I had a little girl and asked if he would let the two families know. No Nyoongar in Pinjarra had a phone in their house so the police sergeant was the best option for me to get a message to family. He must have told them because I received a telegram from my mum sending her love and saying she was glad I now had a girl. Jason also left a message that he would be coming up that afternoon to visit me and to meet his daughter.

I waited all day. No visit. No phone call. Nothing. Around seven o'clock that evening I was in tears when the nurse asked if I could walk to the desk and talk to someone on their phone. Jason was on the line and I ripped into him. Never mind that the nurse was listening, I busted him with some choice words.

When I had calmed down, he said that he had, in fact, come up to the hospital with his mum. However, when they asked at the front desk for me, they were told by staff that I was not there and I had been released from hospital with my new baby earlier in the day. So Jason and his mum had left. They didn't think about double-checking, or going to the ward and asking for me. Like a lot of our people they wouldn't challenge the word of those in authority.

Jason told me that they were now back in Medina with our two boys. Still angry and upset, I made a point of checking with the duty nurse about the misinformation given to Jason. Was there a mention on the books of me being released that morning? Nothing. The duty nurse apologised over and over and said she had only just started her shift that afternoon, so someone from the morning shift was responsible for the blunder. She promised she would definitely look into it and let me know. But for the remainder of my stay I never heard anything. There was no apology from those responsible.

Well, Jason and his mum came back within the hour, a bit after visiting hours, but the duty nurse let them stay for a full hour. My baby girl met her dad and Nanna Edna for the first time. Like me, they couldn't get over how beautiful our baby girl was and being her dad, Jason got to choose her name.

He explained that as a young bloke out riding a horse rounding up cattle in Mogumber Mission, he had come across a lonely grave with only one name on a wooden cross – Alison. He said it touched his heart and he vowed then and there to name his first girl child Alison. So the three of us welcomed Miss Alison Lavinia Kagan into our lives.

The following Saturday morning Jason and his mum came to the hospital in the car. In keeping with hospital practice, one nurse *pushed me to the car in a wheelchair and another* other carried baby Alison. Once we were settled in, the nurses gave a quick wave and went back into the hospital. I thought we would take straight off for home.

Nothing doing. When Jason didn't start the car I asked him what was wrong. What was the hold-up? He explained the back tyre was absolutely flat and we had no spare. Next minute, without saying a word, Jason got out of the driver's seat, walked to the boot and took out two car jacks. One he put under our car and once it was up, he took the flat tyre off. He then put the other jack under the car parked next to ours and raised that tyre. He swapped tyres and we drove off. His mum kept looking back all the way to Fremantle. I think she was worried the police would come looking for us and arrest her son. But luck was with us and we got home safe.

After Alison was born, life in Medina continued much as before. The only thing different was it seemed Jason was spending more time than ever at the pub. My hands were full with my two boys and our new baby girl so I wasn't really keeping tabs on what he was doing. As well, I was breastfeeding and that often left me quite tired. I would fall asleep early in the afternoon for an hour or so. My boys had a nap too, so we could all get through the rest of our day. Like my mum did with Dad, I made sure that there was a feed when Jason knocked off work. After supper, we would all watch television together for a while. But more often than not, after checking we were okay, he'd head out leaving me and our kids at home.

There were other times though when, as a young family, we went for the weekend to Pinjarra and spent a couple of days with family. They all adored our beautiful little blonde baby girl. Her two brothers were very possessive of her. For some reason they got upset when certain little cousins wanted to nurse her. They were fine with some of their older cousins, but the minute others wanted to hold Alison, they kicked up a real fuss.

Around this time my friend Isla asked if I was interested in going to church in Pinjarra with a Christian group from Armadale. Their group was neither Anglican nor Catholic but a new denomination none of us had heard about. There were four or five 'Brothers of the Church' and they would come around in a twelve-seater bus and pick up people from the Medina and Mandurah areas. They would then travel to Pinjarra to their church for Sunday worship. I thought I would give it a try – and it would get me and the kids out of the house for a while. I'd always had religion in my life thanks to Mum and Dad and my sister Lucy, so that part was no problem. It was arranged that the church brothers would pick us up the following Sunday morning at ten o'clock.

When Sunday rolled around, the four of us were dressed and ready to go. When they pulled up, I saw Isla was already in the bus, along with about six other people. I was pleasantly surprised at how casual and easygoing it turned out. The two boys behaved themselves all the way to Pinjarra. The big windows on the bus allowed them to look out and see everything, so they really enjoyed the ride.

Over the next few months sometimes we would stay down in Pinjarra and visit with family for the afternoon. When that happened, Leira would drive the kids and me back to Medina. She was living and working in Perth so it worked out for all of us. Jason never came to church, but that suited him because he would spend his Sunday watching television and recuperating from boozing the night before. One good thing was that whenever Leira dropped us off, he would usually have supper cooked and she would have a feed with us before heading further north.

BUSH BASH FIGHTS

The weekly fights started at the pub in Medina around this time. Jason would go to his team darts on Tuesday, and a few other nights just for a drink, but come the weekend the pub dart challenge for money would be on. He was a pretty good player and most times would bring extra money home from his dart winnings. Somehow, the dart competition escalated to winning fist fights when someone swore at him and called him a nigger. Jason knocked that bloke out. That was it. He was getting challenged to a fight nearly every weekend. He never once came home hurt or injured, but it was still a worry for me.

They didn't always fight in the pub either. The challenge might start there, but then they would line up in the park or head to the Nyoongars' boozing ground in the bush, just out of town. They would light a fire and sit around drinking and carrying on. It was away from residential areas so they could make as much noise as they wanted. It was also well away from the police.

There was one Nyoongar bloke in particular – Benny. He wanted to fight Jason all the time. We thought he would have had enough after he had been knocked out by Jason on a couple of occasions. Not so. That bloke then got other people to challenge Jason. I thought it was ridiculous, but Jason told me if anyone hit him, then he would hit back.

One particular Saturday night, I opened the door for Jason. There he stood all covered in blood. I screamed and nearly fainted with shock. In a panic, I led him to the bathroom and started washing the blood off his face. No cuts. I checked his head. No wound there.

I shouted at him, 'Where are you hurt?'

He said, 'It's not my blood, it's the other bloke's and he's in the car. Can we help him, Lavinia?'

I was stunned. So Jason beats this bloke in a fight, then brings the poor bastard home to our place to look after him. What the hell?

Jason helped the bloke inside and sat him at the kitchen table. I was shocked at what I saw. The bloke's lip was cut, both eyes were cut and he looked terrible. Blood was all over his clothes. Compared to Jason, this fulla was a really big bloke – over six foot three at least, and carrying a bit of weight with him.

Jason took him into the bathroom and turned the shower on him. I grabbed a clean towel, then I found bandaids, bandages and a clean t-shirt. After he'd cleaned him up, Jason shared his food with the bloke and got him a cup of coffee. He then put a mattress on the floor in the lounge and told him to have a rest. They'd talk in the morning. He did tell us his name was Donny Champ. He sure didn't look like a champ that night.

I put the kettle on to make myself a cup of tea. I didn't realise it, but I was shaking uncontrollably. Seeing Jason covered in blood had brought back a terrible memory of something that happened when I was nine years old. Standing in the kitchen, I suddenly felt queasy and grabbed a chair to steady myself. Jason noticed and asked if I was alright. Then I started to cry. Jason pulled up a chair next to me and asked again if I was okay. I shook my head, wiped my eyes and then got up to make myself a cuppa. I told him what I had witnessed as a child.

One night, after an afternoon of heavy drinking, a fight broke out at Uncle Levi and Aunty May's place. From our place, we could hear the swearing, screaming and smashing of bottles. Their dogs were barking so loud it sounded like those dwerts were going mad.

Suddenly we could hear people running over, calling for help. Mum said, 'That's May. It sounds like one of her boys is with her.'

Mum moved to open the front door, but Dad said to leave it closed. If someone was chasing them, they would see the light streaming through the front door and follow them to our place. So Mum sent Trevor and Edwin to go out the back door and bring whoever it was being chased around to the back of our house.

My sisters Rita and Hannah and I were all sitting on beds in the back room straining our ears, listening to what Mum and Dad were saying. When we heard our brothers bring some people to the back door, we felt afraid, but being stickybeaks we got up to have a look.

Just as we opened our bedroom door, they entered through the back door. Aunty May was covered in blood. There was a gash on her forehead, another one on the top of her head. She was bleeding from her mouth and she could barely see out of her battered eyes. Her son, our cousin Isaac, was bleeding profusely from a wound to his head.

Rita dragged Hannah and me back into our room, but it was too late. We had already seen our beloved aunty damaged and bleeding. She could barely stay conscious. Thankfully, Isaac, being a strong young bloke, had virtually carried his mother the four hundred yards to our place, though he had already taken a battering himself. He too was covered in blood and had collapsed on the kitchen floor now that he knew Aunty May was safe. Mum sent my two brothers to get the police. In the meantime, Rita, being a trained nurse, bandaged the head wounds with strips torn from a sheet. This slowed the blood flow. Hannah and I were crying because we thought they would surely die. Mum ordered us to get to bed.

When the police finally came to take Aunty May to hospital, they questioned Dad and Mum about what had happened. Mum told them as much as they knew. They found out later that those three men, in-laws to one of Aunty May's daughters, had come to visit their brother. When Uncle Levi and his other sons had gone to town to get more booze, for some reason those three drunken mongrels had started on Aunty May and Isaac. As a young girl I was not told the reason why they had been fighting, but to see my aunty and cousin hurt so badly will stay with me forever.

Aunty May told the police that as well as punching and kicking them, those bastards had hit her with a heavy lantern, and both she and Isaac had been hit with a small axe. The police ended up catching those three a few weeks later and they were jailed for years. Jason's turning up at our house all covered in blood brought back the memory of what I had seen that night with Aunty May and Isaac.

Jason and I yarned for a quite a while and I calmed down. But I still found it very difficult to go to sleep that night. The next day we found out the bloke Jason had fought with was from Kalgoorlie and had a bit of a reputation as a fighter. Benny, the Nyoongar bloke who was getting people in to fight Jason, had paid big Donny to fight him. When the big bloke got a hiding, his new friend Benny took off and left him out there. After that, Jason and big Donny became really good friends.

MEETING THE NEW MUNARTJ

Life continued much the same in Medina as it did before Alison was born. Somehow, we managed to save enough to buy a new motor car, which helped us a whole lot. Up until then, we usually walked to the shops and got a taxi home with our groceries. We were fortunate enough to have our milk and bread delivered, and there was also a travelling greengrocer who came past our house once a week selling fruit and vegetables. Our accounts with those who made the deliveries was paid up each payday, so we always had food in the house for our little ones. But it felt so good to just jump into our car and go to the shops.

I didn't have a driver's licence yet, so Jason did all the driving on the rare occasions we went on a family outing. On weekends he still went to the pub, but he would walk down and leave the car at home. He needed his driver's licence for work and didn't want to risk getting booked for drunk driving. The police had booked a number of our friends and relatives for driving while drunk. Losing his right to drive wasn't an option, so Jason did the right thing and walked to the pub.

The local sergeant, 'Old Bluey' Gray, knew just about everyone who lived in Medina. He had worked in country towns in the Mid West so he had a lot of experience dealing with our lot. He gave us Nyoongars a fair go, but would not tolerate anyone breaking the law. Not everyone liked him, but they all respected him. He learned the name of all the Nyoongars living in 'his' area, not just those he accommodated in the cell overnight for being too drunk and on the streets. He also knew some of the oldies from past encounters in the country.

My uncle Dave was one of those and he introduced me to Old Bluey one day at the local shops. Sergeant Gray was a burly, ruddy-looking bloke and I could easily imagine him as Santa. Just stick a red suit and a white beard on him. Everything else was already there, built in. The big round belly, the red cheeks, the white hair and the booming laugh.

Sergeant Gray never bothered the boozers at the bush bash outside of town. At first, it was only the blokes and they bought a few cartons and flagons and headed there to finish off their Friday nights before heading home. I don't know if he knew about the fights, but if he did, there was never anyone arrested for it.

There was this one time, though, when the local drinkers gathered in a park area that was referred to by Nyoongars as Medina Hill. They were drunk, kicking up a fuss and making a lot of noise so it was reported to Sergeant Gray. He sent his two young constables to pick them up and bring them to the lock-up. When they got to the rowdy mob, the young officers ordered everyone into the back of the paddy wagon. The boozers got in, all the while drunkenly complaining of police harassment and colour prejudice towards Nyoongars. The one exception was a bloke who had fallen asleep.

The two young cops got hold of him by his shoulders and his boots and, without ceremony, tossed him in with the others. They locked the back door of the paddy wagon with a resounding bang, shouting loudly for everyone to shut up.

Next minute, they could hear a big kerfuffle in the back. Before they even pulled off, the other men had their faces pressed against the barred windows gasping for breath.

'Let us out, Boss. We can't breathe, we need fresh air, please! You killing us. Let us out! God watching you nasty bastards.'

They were all screaming out, begging for fresh air.

Apparently the sleeping bloke the police put into the vehicle had shit himself in the worst way. The night before he had tucked into a big feed of curried kangaroo meat. Fuelled by cheap wine, goona had run all over his pants, down to his boots and out onto the floor of the police van. It reeked to high heaven in that confined space!

All the way to the police station the other poor buggers moved as far away from him as they could, holding their shirts over their heads, pressing the material into their mouths. Some gagging so badly tears came to their eyes.

When they got to the police station and the back door of the van was finally opened, they were pushing each other out of the way, choking and vomiting and stepping straight over their stinking mate who was still lying there. They just about ran into the police station still gasping for fresh air.

They called their drinking mate some pretty choice words. Then they combined these with every swear word they ever learned and could remember, and even some new ones. Old Bluey could be heard way down the streets of Medina, laughing his head off. It was a month or so before anyone went drinking back on the hill.

HAUNTED

Alison was one and half when I found out I was pregnant with our fourth child. I was a bit surprised because I was breastfeeding her and according to the old wives' tales, it was more difficult to get boodjari. So much for that. But I was happy that there would be another baby, even though I was still spending a lot of time at home with just me, my two boys and Alison every weekend.

Then I began to notice a few more strange things that happened around our home. Doors opening by themselves, and lights coming on when no one was in the room. I had always felt the house was haunted but now it seemed to be getting worse, as if the ghost was upset about something. Whatever it was, she made her presence felt more often, and even stronger, to a number of people. One time, my mum was staying with us and was awakened by an invisible someone pulling the blankets off her from the foot of the bed. Mum sat straight up and shouted, 'Fuck off!' Immediately, the blanket pulling stopped. Mum got up and, still swearing very loudly, switched on the light.

All the shouting and swearing woke us up. Jason and I went to see what was happening. Mum was angry and really shaken up by that spirit. She moved her mattress into the lounge room and turned the television on. We sat up talking with her for a long while. I made a cuppa and she chain-smoked about four cigarettes before she finally settled down. That night, all the lights were left on until the next morning.

Another time, my mum-in-law fell asleep in the lounge room while watching television. She woke up to see a pale, ghostly female figure standing there staring right at her. The old girl screamed and started swearing out loud, got up and banged so loudly on our bedroom door I think she woke up the neighbours. After that, nobody except the little ones went back to sleep. Again, every light in the house was switched on and left on.

The hauntings got so bad I had a word to Mrs Cray, our Native Welfare officer, when she came to check on me and my family in her fortnightly rounds. I told her we were not getting any rest and I was really struggling. I could never get a good night's sleep and I seemed to be tired all the time.

I told Mrs Cray that our families in Pinjarra had promised to send an old spiritual man to smoke the place out and get rid of the ghost, but it never happened. Instead, Mrs Cray organised for the University of Western Australia to send a team out to our house to investigate the ghostly sightings. They came out with some weird-looking electric gadgets and over a couple of days spent a lot of time doing all sorts of tests. Their tests definitely showed a presence there. Well hello! We knew that already! Some of us had actually seen her. Could they get rid of her? No, they couldn't. Thanks for nothing. My Uncle Alfonso, a devout Catholic, suggested we get a priest in and bless the place. My family again suggested we get our house smoked the traditional Nyoongar way. We did it all, but nothing seemed to deter the ghost. She wasn't moving for anyone or anything.

When I mentioned it to Uncle David, he recalled that some years before we moved into the Medina area, there had been a house fire and a woman and a little girl had died in the blaze. He said her other two children had gotten out safely. Uncle David suggested that maybe our house was built over the one that had been burnt to the ground and she had come back looking for her other two kids. It didn't put my mind at ease in any way, but that explained why my young nieces would not sleep in the lounge whenever they visited. They had seen her one night leaning right over them when they were lying in front of the television. Since then, a bed had to be made for them on the floor in my bedroom.

During this time, even on some weekdays, Jason seemed to be spending more and more time away from home. I told him about *the unexplained happenings but I'm not sure he believed me.* The ghost didn't seem to bother him. And why should it? He was hardly there and each time he wasn't with us, I would block the door.

Almost every weekend I would be by myself with my three kids and an ever-growing belly. Sometimes with visitors. And always with the ghost.

It got so bad that whenever I went to bed, I would take food, water, a torch and my Bible, and lock us all in the room for the night. Even though I had a big baby-growing belly, I would push the wardrobe against the bedroom door and not move until daylight. The bedroom light, too, would be left on all night.

Luckily, I was still able to breastfeed Alison, so I didn't have to get up to make a bottle for her. I didn't want to risk the possibility of seeing our unwanted guest. It got so bad that on the rare nights when Jason decided to come home early, that would be the only time I left our room – to let him in. More often than not, he didn't turn up until the next day and the kids and I would spend the whole night alone.

I felt like I was in survival mode and I had to protect my children and myself. It was a real struggle for me to follow this process, but I did it every weekend for months. Towards the end of my pregnancy, I started spending more and more time in Pinjarra, staying with my in-laws and catching up with my parents. That way I had company. And my mother was close by.

I reckon some people must have thought I was a bit crazy for going back to Pinjarra every weekend. After all, we lived across the road from the maternity hospital in Medina and I was being treated by my local Medina doctor. However, I took the precaution of visiting our doctor in Pinjarra and booking a bed in that local hospital. Leira was in Pinjarra most weekends and either she or my brother-in-law Tedo would be able to drive me to hospital if my baby happened to come along.

NEW LITTLE KOORDAH

It was a Sunday, very early in February 1972, and the weather was really hot and muggy. Two potential cyclones were brewing off the North West in the Pilbara and their effects were being felt all the way down the coast. The heat was oppressive, so at around seven o'clock that morning I had a shower to cool my swollen body down. As I was dressing, the first signs began telling me that my baby was ready to be born. There was a slight niggle in my lower belly and in the mirror I could see it had dropped. Then small smears of blood appeared on my knickers. Though there was no pain, I knew it was time. I had brought my 'hospital baby bag' with me so I could have gone straight across to the maternity ward at the Pinjarra hospital.

The inner voice that has been guiding me since I was a young child told me I had to go to King Edward hospital. Twenty minutes later when Leira got up, I asked if she could take me up to Subiaco. She asked, really gently, why not go across to the hospital in Pinjarra? No, I insisted, I have to get to King Edward. She was a bit worried. Her main concern being the radiator on her old car was playing up. We could get about ten miles, but would need to stop and fill it up before it overheated.

Just then, my brother-in-law Tedo turned up and somewhat reluctantly said he would come company with us two women. My three little ones would stay with their grandparents. Everything was hastily organised, with bottles and bottles of water in the back seat of the car next to me, and Leira and Tedo sitting in the front. Sure enough, we made it about ten kilometres to the Serpentine Bridge before we had to refill the radiator with water and black pepper.

While they were attending to the radiator, I got my first real contraction. It was only a small twinge, but just as they got back in the car I groaned. Leira and Tedo looked horrified. They nearly turned white. I think if I wasn't in pain, I would have laughed. As it was, we got under way again quick smart.

We made it right through Mandurah and got a good distance before we had to pull up again. My second and third pains came about twenty minutes apart. We had the urge to speed to get me to the hospital, yet if the old car was pushed too hard, it would get too hot, too soon, and we would get nowhere. Three stressed young Nyoongars is not a pretty sight. Funny, but definitely not pretty.

I can only believe that the old spirits must have been looking after us that Sunday. Leira had pulled into the service station halfway between Mandurah and Medina, to check the radiator. Just as we were parked there, my sister Hannah and her husband, Nicky, pulled up in their brand-new blue Ford ute. Hannah, who was a few months pregnant, and Nicky were on their way to visit Mum and Dad in Pinjarra. She casually walked over to say hello, but then Leira told her what was happening.

Well, she and Nicky decided to transfer me to their car and told Leira they would take me the rest of the way to the hospital. I don't know who was more relieved – Leira, Tedo, Hannah or me.

Once we got underway in the new-beaut ute, I sort of relaxed a bit. It was agreed that we would pull into Medina and pick Jason up to be company for me at the maternity hospital, so we made the detour. He too asked if I wanted to go to the hospital in Medina. Again I refused and insisted I had to go to King Edward for my baby's birth. The journey would have been pretty straightforward except every time I groaned with a contraction, Nicky panicked. He started yelling at Hannah to do something. What could she do?

After what seemed an eternity, catching every red light possible, we finally arrived at the hospital and Nicky drove straight to the ambulance entrance. He ran and got a wheelchair while Jason and Hannah helped me exit the ute. I was glad Jason insisted he push me. My pains were getting stronger and closer together and suddenly the stress of everything was beginning to get to me.

Once through reception, I was taken straight to the delivery ward. After I was settled in by nursing staff, I asked Jason to go back with Hannah and Nicky and be with our kids in Pinjarra. They had done their bit to get me to the hospital safe and reasonably sound. From here on in, it was up to the medical professionals and me. Even though my labour pains were much stronger, and now only a few minutes apart, I was very happy that my old Nyoongar spirits had guided me to King Edward and I know that it was the place I was meant to be. For both me and my baby's sake.

This delivery was not like any of my other children. After I arrived at the hospital my contractions had gone on all day. I was feeling tired and towards evening, as my strength waned, the pain and stress became almost unbearable. All the medical indicators showed that the strain was too much on my heart, and I could tell there was something amiss with my baby as well. In whispered tones the delivery ward team called in their specialists. The decision was made by the head doctor. I would have a caesarean delivery.

I felt so bad, the thought crossed my mind that maybe I was dying. Through extremely tired eyes I remember the nurses reading out the words and then I signed the permission sheet for them to proceed. Shortly after, they gave me some anesthetic and I went out like a light.

I found myself floating, looking down on the doctors operating on me. I saw them cut me open. I saw my baby being born – a third boy. He was taken from my sleeping body, and transferred to a small table about two yards away from where my body was still lying on the operating table.

From my vantage point near the ceiling, my spirit could see that only one doctor and one nurse was still with my sleeping body. The doctor was starting to stitch me up. The six or so others were all gathered around my baby, talking agitatedly in hushed tones. Nurses moving from table to table with instruments. Something was terribly, terribly wrong.

In a flash, my spirit went straight back into my body. Midway through having my belly stitched, I stirred, then sat bolt upright. I screamed out loud, 'What's wrong with my baby boy? There's something wrong, I saw it!'

I shouted so loudly everybody in the room was shocked. But their priority was still my baby. The team of six or more only gave me one quick glance before focusing back on tending to his tiny brown body. The nurse gently tried to push me back down, explaining that she and the doctor needed to finish helping me. They needed to close the incision. The doctor nearest to me insisted quite loudly to anyone listening, 'That shouldn't have happened. I gave her enough anesthetic to last the whole time. She should have slept right through. How did she know she had a baby boy?'

Reluctantly, I lay back, wide awake now. Fear for my boy and his little life took over and I started to cry. The anesthetist carefully put a mask over my nose, telling me my baby would be alright. He said for me to breathe, everything will be okay. Finally, lights out completely.

I woke sometime later, still in the delivery room. I looked around for my boy. The doctor told me he had been taken to the Neonatal Intensive Care Unit. There were serious complications, but he was okay. Again the tears came but they were tinged with relief. I had been right to insist that I come to King Edward. My baby was okay. That's all I needed to hear. He would be alright.

I didn't get to see my baby boy until an hour later. By that time I'd had a short sleep and eaten a small meal. Still very weak, I was taken by wheelchair so I could at least see him through the glass windows. My son was attached to all sorts of wires and monitors, and he had tubes in his little nose and mouth.

I could see he was a big baby. They said he weighed in at ten pounds fifteen ounces. My son had masses of long, straight, jet-black hair and the chubbiest brown face ever. His eyes were closed, but the nurse told me they were very dark too. He was beautiful. I loved him and I loved his strong spirit.

In order to get closer to him I had to don a new gown, mask and gloves. I was wheeled into the room and put next to his closed-in crib – an incubator, one of the nurses told me. There was an opening on the side for whenever nurses needed to treat him. I was told by the nurses I was not to touch him. But I took a glove off and reached in and put my bare finger into his tiny little hand.

His baby fingers closed strongly around my finger and my heart melted right there and then. I knew in my very soul whatever was wrong with him, he would pull through it.

After ten minutes, they pushed me back to my ward. Later on, the doctor came and explained that my son had been born with a hole in his heart. He drew some diagrams for me so that I fully understood how serious it was. My baby also had an extra bone in his upper body which meant he had one shoulder higher than the other. For me, a twenty-one-year-old Nyoongar woman, it was a lot to take in, but I had an overwhelming belief and faith in God and the old Nyoongar spirits. They had led me to doctors who had expertise and knowledge. Those doctors had helped me and my baby son to come through it all. I gave thanks to God for my little boy's safe delivery.

The doctors told me they would keep him in hospital until his condition stabilised. They also said I would have to give him a whole lot of attention when he came home. He would need round-the-clock medication and care to keep his heart rate steady. I didn't know how I was going to do it with three other young children, but I would have to manage somehow.

Later on, a social worker attached to the hospital came and quizzed me about our home situation. Being a Nyoongar, there was always some question about our capabilities to look after our children. I know they would have put him with a wadjerlar family. Native Welfare would and could foster him out. I made up my mind right then, I was not going to let that happen. He was mine and I wasn't about to let him go to any white family. I asked the social worker to contact Mrs Cray because I knew she would attest to me being a good mother.

FOUR BIRTHDAYS

Being in a big city hospital, I didn't get many visits from my family. From time to time, Jason, Leira, Hannah and Nicky came to check on us and brought me up to speed on all the family and Nyoongar gossip. But everyone was getting on with their usual things and the two weeks I spent in there seemed to pass quickly.

With everything that was going on, I had not given my baby a name. He went for ten days before I named him Shane Cagney Kagan. It suited him to a tee and his Nanna Edna was pleased with his name because her cousin was also a Shane. The name Cagney was after the actor James Cagney, whose film characters always appeared as the tough guy.

I knew from the start of his life that my baby boy was already one tough little guy. A little Nyoongar warrior. He needed to be strong; his battles were just beginning.

After nearly three weeks I was deemed well enough to be discharged, but I couldn't take Shane with me. It was one of the hardest things I have ever had to do. I felt gutted, knowing I had to leave my baby behind while I went home.

During those three weeks in hospital, the doctors had removed the tubes from Shane, and I was able to start breastfeeding him. I think that was the reason I was allowed to stay longer in hospital. They said breastmilk would be of great benefit to him at that young age, considering the seriousness of his heart condition. All the natural defences and antibodies of my breastmilk could only strengthen him.

My discharge day arrived and Jason came by bus to pick me up. No motor car this time. He told me our vehicle had been in an accident and was in the garage getting fixed. Tedo had borrowed the car and been smoking a cigarette while he was driving. Unfortunately, he only had shorts on and when a sharp gust of wind blew hot cigarette ash onto his bare legs, just near his important parts, it burnt him badly.

We were told by others in the car with him, that he screamed like a girl, then cursed. He took his eyes off the road for only a second to brush the hot ash away from his crotch and promptly crashed into a light pole. Luckily, apart from the burns, he wasn't hurt, but it badly damaged the radiator. So now our family was back to walking, pushing prams and catching buses and taxis for a while.

Jason and I took the train to Fremantle and caught the last bus to Medina. It was a very emotional time for me to leave my baby behind and head home. I could see it was hard for Jason too. In all our time together, I think that was the closest we ever got as a couple. We shared in the sadness of having to leave our little boy behind. He tried to ease my pain and cheer me up by saying Shane would be okay, the doctors know what they are doing. He reminded me that our other kids would be glad to have me home again. They were not too keen on his cooking. Thinking about them helped; it put a stop to the tears and we made some plans to tell them all about their new brother.

At times over the next few months, things got really tough for the family. The continual caring for the three little ones at home while trying to get up to see Shane at the hospital was hard. As luck would have it, when I got back home Alison took straight to being breastfed again. I was making so much milk I had to feed her, so I didn't get breastmilk sickness. It really was a tremendous help because I could feed Ali, then head up to see Shane and give him a feed as well.

The hospital staff were pretty flexible and I was able to see my boy every day if and when I could get up to King Edward. Sometimes that was after Jason got home from work. We'd borrow a friend's car, drive up there and see him outside normal visiting hours. I was making so much breastmilk, I felt like a Jersey cow.

Each time I was at the hospital, I would use a breast pump and get out enough breastmilk to last him two or three feeds overnight. It worked out that going up every second day was better, though I missed being with my baby.

Six long weeks passed and I was so worried about how much longer he might be kept there. Was he ever going to be allowed to come home? I asked Mrs Cray if she could find out anything.

Finally, after two and a half months, our boy was allowed to come home. The doctors had worked out his medications and noted that he was progressing really well. After meeting with us and Mrs Cray to talk about what we had to do once he was home, Shane was released and into our care. Thankfully our car was fixed by that time, so we took him home to Medina in style. Bringing him home turned out to be a bit of a celebration. Family had turned up to meet their new little relative and bought a cake and some cool drinks.

His three siblings were so excited. Of course they all had to take a turn to nurse him. Big brother Jason was first, Aimon was second and when eighteen-month-old Alison got him, she wouldn't give him up – not without two slices of cake and some serious coaxing and bribery on our part.

For the first month, I don't think either one of us parents got a decent sleep. We were so scared of something going wrong. We had to give Shane his heart medicine every four hours on the hour. It had to be the absolute correct amount. Too much would make his little koort race, not enough would make it too slow. Either way, it would not be good for him and the consequences were deadly.

Everyone in the family helped to take care of Shane. Jason Junior, Aimon and Alison loved their baby brother and were always looking out for him. Alison was especially protective of him. She was a real little woman-head looking after him from the time they woke up each morning until he took a nap.

In the first couple of years, he had to go back to into hospital quite a few times. Sometimes it was to avoid more serious medical complications if he had a bad cold or teething problems.

Whenever that happened, Alison would get back on mimmi and keep the milk flowing. But as soon as Shane came home she gave way to her baby brother. My beautiful, kind-hearted girl never once complained about it. I think that special bond between them has never been broken, even as adults.

On his first birthday, we had another very special celebration. It was a real milestone in his little life. He loved it. We loved it. So much so that from then on Shane celebrated his birthday four times a year, every year until way after he started school. He would have his own cake with candles on his birthday in February. Next, he would have his own cake alongside his brother Jason's birthday cake in March. Then it was with Alison in July and again with Aimon in August. It became a family tradition that continued until he was about seven.

The other three never complained or worried about sharing their special day with him. It was like they knew how lucky we were to have him with us. Shane was their precious baby brother. God's gift to our family. They shared everything with him, they protected him, they cared for him and they totally loved him.

TIME FOR A CHANGE

On the surface, everything in our lives seemed okay. Both Jason and I were making a concerted effort to take care of Shane. Jason would come home straight after work and help me with the three older kids and do things around our house. He even did some of the cooking. It was really good to have him home, especially at night because I could tend to Shane knowing he would look after the other three if needed. At first it was hard going having to give Shane his medicine every four hours on the hour. Also, I could shout out to Jason if I sensed that ghost was around during night time. Although Jason told me he hadn't seen the ghost, he did say he believed it was there. Too many other people, including his mother and my mother had encountered her.

But after about four months, Jason would stay out longer, and he began to mix with a different crowd. Before, it was just going to darts two evenings a week with his workmates. He would get back home reasonably early in the evening. That was still happening. But then I noticed when he went to the pub on the Friday, he was beginning to stay out for the whole weekend.

I found myself getting really angry with Jason and it was a real worry for me because it meant I couldn't get much of a rest. When he wasn't home at night, I made sure the kids and I were secure in our haunted house. I bolted all the doors and windows and pushed the wardrobe across our bedroom door as I had always done.

The light was also left on all night. Medina didn't have a high crime rate, but any uninvited living visitors who did get in would have to deal with the ghost by themselves. If she didn't deter them and they tried to get into our room, my weapons were lined up right near the door, starting with the trusty softball bat which was given to me by one of my cousins. She said I might need it, and I was prepared to use it.

News filtered back to me through the Nyoongar grapevine that now both men and women were going out to the local bush bash after the pub, lighting a big fire and hanging out there. Sometimes until daylight. The fact that the blokes had changed their self-imposed rule about women not being included there meant nothing to me. There was no way I could or would join them. For me, my children were my priority, so going out to the bush bash was never going to happen. However, it didn't stop Jason from heading out there every weekend, carton of beer in hand.

I think that's where his 'affair' or 'fucking around' or whatever it was started. Maybe it was out of his own sense of guilt, but Jason would come home either charged up or with a hangover, accusing me of running around behind his back. Totally confused, I asked where he got his information from and how could he even think such a thing. He said his informant was a very reliable source. Of course, he didn't say who told him. He did say he would kill me if he ever found out it was true. Usually, after claims and counterclaims, things would settle down, mostly for the kids' sake. They didn't need to see their parents arguing. I had had enough of witnessing violence and seeing my relatives arguing and fighting with each other when I was a kid.

However, Jason's accusations sparked my curiosity and I began asking my Medina mob if they knew anything. The only information I ever got was that a Nyoongar woman who lived up near Fremantle was jirripin around for him. Always flirting with him. No names, though. The bush-bash fullas had closed ranks. Or maybe the people I asked didn't have anything to do with those lot going out to the bush bash and getting drunk every weekend.

Either way, I could not find out anything. As expected, when I did mention it to him when he was sober, Jason denied everything. He said I had nothing to worry about. My focus was on our four children, I couldn't do much else other than believe him. Our little ones needed my constant attention, and there was no way I could leave them just to follow their father around monitoring his movements and worrying about the people, including the women, with whom he was mixing.

A pattern had developed. During the week, everything was okay. Come the weekend, he'd be gone again. When he got home, the accusations against me would start. We would end up arguing, but there was no physical violence involved. This went on for months and I didn't know what to do about the situation except put up with it. The kids and I were going to Pinjarra more and more on the weekends and staying with the oldies. It seemed a safer place and I got some mental and physical rest. Or Nanna Edna would come and spend time with us. Sometimes even Jason's dad came up to Medina to catch up with his grannies.

When that happened, we would be like the 'happy family'. Then Jason was the perfect husband and dad. When the oldies weren't around though, the boozing, bush-bashing nights and accusations aimed at me continued. In an effort to get to bottom of all these changes in Jason and in our marriage, I still asked around whenever I caught up with my lot, if they knew anything, to no avail.

One dear old aunty did offer me insight, though. 'I tell you now, niece. When a man comes home accusing you of running around with other men, you can bet he's the one who's been sleeping with another woman. That's our Nyoongar mans for you. That's their stupid bloody ways. I reckon your man trying to put his guilt on to you. He trying to hide his doing wrong by blaming you for messing with somebody else. Don't worry, my girl, it will all come out one day. Nyoongars can't keep their big mouths shut for too long. You'll find out, Lavinia, you see. Coming back blaming you all the time. Fuck that! And fuck him! Why don't you leave the arsehole, my girl?'

I couldn't answer my old aunty. There was no answer. I had four young children, one with very serious health problems. I couldn't leave. I couldn't just turn my back and walk away. I felt utterly powerless, but I had to get my priorities right. The other thing was – where would I go anyway?

The final time the drunken accusations happened, I didn't expect it to turn violent. I was up, having just given Shane a feed. Jason came home drunk and started in on me again, his loud voice making Shane cry. This time he gripped me by my shirt front with his left hand, his knuckles digging into my throat. He shouted right into my face, swearing at me.

'You cunt, you been running round behind my back! They told me. Who is he?'

Then, with his right fist, he gave me a short hard jab in my stomach causing me to double up. Still I held tightly to baby Shane. I didn't want to drop him. On straightening up, I was utterly shocked. Winded and scared, at first I couldn't talk. I knew what he could do with his fists. I had seen the blokes twice his size he'd belted and left lying in a pool of blood.

Still, I stood my ground. I looked him straight in the eye and shouted back at him, saying he was getting me confused with the sluts he was drinking around with. I knew I was taking a huge risk, but I had to talk up against his accusations. What made it worse is that all this time I was holding Shane, trying to settle him down.

Physically, I couldn't defend myself. My arms were around my little boy and I wasn't going to let him fall.

I kept looking Jason straight in his eyes, tears forming in mine as I mentally braced myself for the hit. It never came. Instead with a slight shove, he let go of me, turned and sat down on the couch. With his head bowed, it seemed as though he started to realise something. In a quiet voice he said, 'I'm sorry, Lavinia. This is not me. I'm sorry.'

Adrenaline and bravado gone, I slumped onto the nearest kitchen chair, still holding my baby boy very close. My silent tears just kept flowing. I reached for a cloth and wiped my tired face.

For some reason, Shane had stopped crying and was looking up at me. Maybe he had sensed the threat, the tension and my real terror and knew the moment had now passed. His little hand reached up and touched my chin ever so gently and the whole world went silent.

I still don't know what Jason saw in my face that made him stop, but it was enough. I realised our relationship was in real serious trouble. We could not go on this way. I was twenty-two years old, trying to raise four young children virtually by myself. I was under threat of physical violence from my husband of six years and struggling to cope with it all, and I didn't trust him not to hit me again. Something had to give.

The final straw with our living in Medina came a few weeks later. It was a Sunday and I was rushing around getting myself and the children ready to go to church. Finally, we were all fed, washed and dressed. Jason said he would clean up after we left and put supper on for this evening. He and the kids were watching cartoons on television. Everything was packed to go. I opened the front door to put the two small bags holding their nappies and juice on the front porch for when the church bus pulled up.

She was right there. A tall white woman in a long dress and black laced up boots. Standing in full view of me. Staring right at me. That ghost! The woman's spirit was staring right at my face. I dropped both bags, spilling nappies and juice bottles everywhere. I swear I have never screamed as loud or as shrill as I did that day. The woman vanished. Jason and the boys rushed to me, firing questions at me, but I was shaking all over. Jason grabbed me and I clung to him. My legs felt like rubber. I couldn't talk, let alone walk.

All I could do was point to the area where she had been standing. He could see nothing amiss except for our stuff scattered on the front porch. He helped me to the nearest chair. For once, he looked very worried about me. I told him what I had seen and that she had actually showed herself to me. In broad daylight! That was only supposed to happen at night, unna?

With tears flowing from my eyes, I shook my head and I told Jason that ghost could have the place. I was taking my children and leaving this house forever. When the church bus pulled up, my kids and I piled in. It wasn't until half an hour later that I finally calmed down, just as we got to Mandurah.

PEACE OF MIND

It took a few weeks, but everything that belonged to us was taken out of that house. I only went back once to make sure all our important papers and photos were collected and brought down to Pinjarra. We still had debt on the place at Medina, but I didn't care. I was so desperate to leave and not go back, I asked Mum and Dad if I could stay with them at the old place where I had grown up. Only my brother Clem and his wife were living with them at the time, so they gave me the nod to move in. We couldn't move in with my in-laws because they already had Jason's sisters and their families living with them.

So we moved most of our clothes and light furniture into the old place. It was three single beds, mattresses, pillows and sheets and one dressing table. Mum and Dad already had the old place furnished so that was all we really needed. The rooms were rough, but we made do. We had a roof over our heads. There was still no running water or electricity, but there was a wood stove and a kerosene fridge. Most important of all, there was peace.

Jason moved in with us and, much to my surprise, things settled right down. He got a local job and was bringing in good money. Jason had bought a car from one of his mates so we had transport to get things done, and he was coming home and spending more time with us as a family again. He had always gotten on with my parents and Clem, so there was no bad feeling between them.

We applied for another State Housing home and because of Shane's health issues we were given immediate consideration. Priority listing, they told us. We even got written support from our local member of parliament. We were told it still could take some time, but at least we were now on their list.

There weren't too many dramas living at the old place, except when some of our relatives came to visit Mum and Dad and wanted to drink there. Mum usually had a yarn with them for a little while, gave them a feed if they were hungry, and then sent them on their way. For health reasons, even though she liked a nip of wine now and then, Mum wasn't drinking kgaepa or smoking gnummari anymore. Dad had cut right down on his beer drinking too. He still enjoyed a rollie made up of Capstan tobacco though.

Sometimes they would go and stay the weekend in Wattleup with Jono and his family and get dropped off on Sunday night. Either Jono or Dot would bring them home. They'd stay for a feed before driving back. Mum did get a bit concerned when Dot started coming down to Pinjarra during the week and was seen drinking with her relatives. Jono was working and Dot had moved her brothers in with her into the family home in Wattleup, so there was no reason for her to be down in Pinjarra, especially on school days.

I don't know if Mum ever mentioned her concerns to Jono, but she worried what was happening with them because Dot would drive down, sometimes by herself, sometimes with the kids in tow. The main concern was the boozing and driving drunk with kids in the car.

One night, she even turned up at the old place. She was drunk and with her cousins and Jason's nieces. They were shouting and swearing so much Dad soon told them to get on their way or he would send for the police. Jason went out and spoke with them for a few minutes and they took off, taking Dot with them.

Despite incidents like that, I was very grateful to be staying with Mum and Dad because I had peace of mind again. My spirit was happy. I was young and feeling so much better and I managed quite well there.

Carting the water from the well in buckets and lighting our place at night with kerosene lanterns really made me appreciate the things Mum did for us kids when we were young. I didn't care about how flash that other house was with its lovely carpets, blinds, tap water and electricity. That ghost could keep them all!

We stayed there for six months with Mum and Dad before moving in with Jason's parents. Around that time the government had allocated a four-bedroom house right in town to his parents. It was much roomier than the iron-and-tin house they had on the reserve, and way better than the place where they'd first lived in Roe Avenue. Both his sisters and their families had moved into their own places in Pinjarra too, and Leira was living in Perth.

In a way I was sorry to be leaving Mum and Dad's place. But Nanna Edna welcomed us moving in with her. She loved her oldest son and it certainly made some things a lot easier for me and the kids having running water and electricity again.

GOOD THINGS HAPPENING

Soon after we moved back in with his parents, my oldest sister Lucy was employed by Community Health. It was 1974 and we finally had a qualified Nyoongar healthcare worker looking after Nyoongar people in our area. Lucy's role was to act as a liaison between us Nyoongars, local doctors and the Department of Health. It was great because she would come and check on Shane and all the other Nyoongar koolungahs in the town. She also monitored the health of all the oldies in the district. Lucy was a local, knew her job and everyone in the community very well, and was respected by everyone, black and white.

With baby Shane, I also had to keep regular appointments with the specialists in Princess Margaret Children's Hospital in Perth. At least once a month, we had to attend those visits with specialists whether he was sick or not. At a local level an arrangement between the hospital and the Department of Health was made with Lucy's senior officer, the local Community Health nurse, to come out and visit us two or three times a week if anyone was sick.

When Lucy started in that position, she would check on Shane and keep a record of his progress. Sometimes she would time her visits just before lunch, so she could check on Shane, record his health details, then stay for a feed before heading back to work.

At nearly three years old, Shane was really quite healthy, even with the hole in his heart and the physical differences he presented.

He still tried to do everything his bigger brothers did and most times he succeeded too. His sister was his little protector and always worried about him, fussing over him. I still had to give him his medicine every four hours on the hour, but his little body grew and developed at the normal rate. There were a few times I had to take him to the local doctor when he got a cold, or when he was cutting his teeth and got a high temperature. Otherwise, his progress was good considering his heart condition, thank God.

In Pinjarra, my children flourished. In fact, we all seemed a whole lot happier. The older boys were enrolled in school and kindergarten and I spent my days doing housework and looking after the two little ones. Jason managed to make his job as a labourer with a local plumbing company a permanent one, and we settled into a good routine.

Jason joined a local darts team and would play in competitions on Tuesday nights. On the weekend he would sometimes go and have a few drinks, but was usually home soon after the pub closed. Sometimes he would go and stay at his mate's place if it got too late. It saved me driving to pick him up late at night and disturbing the kids.

Other good things were happening for us too. It was while we were at his parents' place we took over the care of another little baby boy. Gary was the only son of one of Jason's nieces. She was very young herself and going through some hard times, so we agreed to keep Gary with us. Otherwise Native Welfare would foster him out to a white family somewhere. All four kids welcomed him as their own baby and fussed over him. Shane now had the role of big brother and was very protective of Gary. Those two became very close, and Alison now had another little koolungah to look after and our two older boys joined the local junior footy club winning fairest and best trophies in their age group. Jason was working full-time and we were paying off our Medina debt with state housing. They told us that having five little ones meant that getting our own home was a step closer.

I got my driver's licence thanks to Mum and Lucy, because they chucked in some money together and got me four lessons with a local driving school. I already knew how to drive, but they wanted me to make it official and legal.

The first three lessons were spent fine-tuning my knowledge of the road rules and getting used to the driving school's small training vehicle. The final lesson included taking my *driving test* with the local policeman sitting in the passenger seat. I passed with flying colours.

Other good things were happening for us. Jason was back playing football and even took on the role of coach when the previous one moved away. His team, the Pinjarra Panthers, were made up of all Nyoongar blokes in the area. He loved it. They were part of the Murray Districts Football Competition and they did very well. Playing football was one thing that brought all our Nyoongar community together.

I was twenty-three, young and optimistic. The struggles we faced in Medina faded into the past. Our lives weren't perfect, but things were moving forward, and it seemed they could only get better.

SORRY TIME

We had been living at Jason's parents' house for a few months. As usual, around seven o'clock in the evening, the family had all settled down to watch television. The dishes had been done and the kids were ready for sleep. Edna was stretched out on the long lounge chair with the television tuned to her favourite channel.

When the ads came on, she told us she was getting pains in her chest area and asked if Jason would get her heart tablets from her room. He had only just left the lounge room when Edna cried out then slumped further into the lounge, as though she had fainted. I screamed out to Jason for help. Together we laid Edna on her back so she could breathe easier. We desperately tried to resuscitate her, with me giving her mouth-to-mouth and Jason applying some pressure on her chest.

Tedo ran out to the neighbour's place and shouted at them to call an ambulance. The hospital was only a kilometre away and the medics arrived within minutes. They took over trying to resuscitate Edna, using all their equipment, but after fifteen minutes or so they stepped back. They told us she had gone into full cardiac arrest. She was gone.

Edna's passing left a huge gap. Jason, his dad and siblings were devastated. She had been the backbone of their family. Jason, Leira and Tedo helped organise their mum's funeral because their dad was too overcome by grief. Edna had been the love of old boy's life and he was completely shattered.

Personally, I had lost a really good friend. She loved Jason, but she had supported both of us so much throughout our marriage. Edna had taught me a lot about being a good mother and wife, and I had never let Jason or the kids down. For that reason alone, I know she respected me.

Following the funeral, it was decided that Jason and I would continue to live at their house to support his dad. He was just on seventy years old and although physically still very independent, he welcomed our company around his home.

BACK INTO SPORT

During this time, I returned to playing sport. When I was living in Medina, before having Shane, I had joined in with other local Nyoongar yorgas, mostly young mums, to form a netball team. We competed in the local competition and our team was made up of both married and single women. It was a lot of fun, and those of us with children could take our kids with us to the local sportsground.

If the weather was wet, then babysitters were found for the hour or so we would be away. If there were no babysitters available, we let the other players know and we stayed home with our own children. It was definitely more social than serious competition, so it didn't matter if we won. Or if we even turned up, because we only needed five players to be there and we could field a team on the courts.

I had my first game of women's basketball around that same time. I had never played the game before in my life. Nearly all our team of Nyoongar netballers decided to give basketball a go too. We called our team the Wildcats Women. My cousin Rick already had a men's basketball team – Wildcats Men – and both teams competed in the inaugural competition in Pinjarra. We only needed five players on each side and that worked for us.

Nobody had a clue about the rules, but it looked simple enough. We were young and reasonably fit, so had a go. Were we in for a shock! Unlike netball, where you were not allowed to walk with the ball, we were allowed to run and bounce the ball up and down the whole court. This one rule alone totally confused us. In our first-ever game, we were thoroughly beaten – sixty points to eight. Well, Nyoongar yorgas walked off shame, some of our teammates swearing about what a poxy game basketball was and vowing never to play it again. Those of us who said we would finish the season took to training two times a week, initially to just learn the game. Also, we had shelled out good money to join so we didn't want to waste that. We were determined to never again be beaten by so many points.

Once we got the hang of it, we never looked back. Sure, sometimes we were beaten, but never by so many points. And we won *a lot of games too. After those wins, we proudly wore the Wildcats* Women tag. The Wildcats Men came and barracked for us each week during the local competition. Some of our Nyoongar fullas even learned the rules properly, got their stripes and umpired local games.

Basketball was in its infancy back then and our teams got to play in a number of competitions throughout the district. Our teams also travelled to basketball carnivals around the South West. The men's team won most of their games and our women's team did really well too. Jason had no interest in playing basketball. He was strictly an Aussie Rules football player and he had his darts. He did support me sometimes by coming along with the kids to watch the local competitions.

After the move back to Pinjarra, I also started playing netball again. This time in a local team which included some of the white girls with whom I had gone to school. Like me, a number of them had young children and it became a family affair on Saturday afternoons at the local netball courts. One day Rick, my young cousin, asked if I would be interested in trying out for a Western Australian Aboriginal netball team. Selectors were holding trials in the metro area to pick a team to travel to a National Aboriginal Sports Carnival in Adelaide. Rick left a pamphlet with all the information about venue, dates and times of the trials. After talking about it with Jason, we decided I should go for it.

With our kids in tow, Jason and I travelled to Fremantle, found the netball courts and I registered with the organisers. After the first day of playing, often in a team with women I did not know, I was asked to come back the next day.

Much to everyone's amazement, I made the final cut of ten players and was given a schedule for training over the next two weeks. There would only be three training sessions during that time.

With family support, I managed to attend each one. An additional surprise came when I was also asked by organisers if I would take on the role of assistant manager for the team. It meant as well as playing I had to attend all administration meetings along with the manager during the carnival.

I was excited and very nervous at the same time. It all seemed a bit overwhelming, especially when I took my first plane ride. I felt so proud to be a part of the team travelling to Adelaide. Our Western Australian Aboriginal Netball team finished second only to the very strong New South Wales team. It was there I was introduced to Mr Charles Perkins, a well-known Aboriginal man who advocated for our rights. And for the first time ever, I heard a young David Gulpilil play the didjeridu to rock'n'roll music. It gave the music a tribal beat and to me, the sound was awesome!

It took a few days for things to settle down at home after all the excitement of the carnival in Adelaide. But with most of us involved in the community and sport we soon were back into a routine of getting on with our lives. Work, school, kindy, doctors' appointments, training, playing footy, basketball, netball and sometimes going bush for picnics on Sundays after church.

The years spent in Medina seemed like a bad dream. Even though we now had five kids to care for, living in Pinjarra with family made it seem effortless. Busy, but there was no real stress. The kids were absolutely blossoming; we were all blossoming. Jason was working full-time, I had my driver's licence and the use of my dad's car to get around.

Mum and Lucy were close by and we caught up nearly every day. I had family support and almost everything was shared, including highlights and sorrows. We were still listed with State Housing to get our own place. In the meantime, life wasn't too bad. It seemed everything was going to work out alright.

KYAH MUM

About a year after Edna had passed away, Lucy expressed some real concern for Mum's health. She had been under the care of her doctor for several years and was on heart medication. Mum was well over sixty and reasonably fit for her age, but the breathlessness she was experiencing was becoming more marked every day.

One day, just after my brother Trevor had gone to court to answer some minor charges, Mum, Hannah and I took off to get lunch for my kids. It was about midday and we were due to meet them at the local youth club hall. I was driving Dad's car with its powerful V8 motor and Mum was sitting in the front seat. When we arrived, I cut the engine, but l left the keys in the ignition. Lucy happened to pull up just behind us in her work car. As usual, she wanted to catch up with us during her lunch hour.

We saw the kids about two streets away running towards us, skylarking as they usually did. They were all in a group coming from school for their lunches. Mum decided she would go and sit in Lucy's work car while I sorted out everyone's lunches. I watched her open her door and step out of Dad's car. Suddenly, she started to gasp, one hand on her chest and one still holding on to the car door.

I jumped out of the driver's seat and ran around to help her. Mum started to collapse, but somehow I was strong enough to pick her up like she was a baby. Mum's head lolled onto my chest. Holding her gently, I placed Mum back into Dad's car. I ran around to start the car and take her to hospital. It would only take a few minutes to get there in Dad's motor. When I looked in the ignition, the keys was not there. Utter panic set in.

Lucy shouted that she would take Mum to the hospital. I lifted Mum and carried her now unconscious body to Lucy's work car. They took off for the hospital, leaving me to frantically search Dad's car inside and out for the missing keys. It was as though they had disappeared into thin air. We never ever did find those of keys.

My kids must have sensed the emergency because they sorted the lunches out for themselves. For the first time ever, there were *no arguments between them. They each* grabbed a lunch pack and quietly headed back to school.

Both Hannah and I were forced to wait until Trevor finally pulled up in a taxi with a spare set of keys from home. One of the other parents had told him what had happened just as he came out of court and he had gone straight home and grabbed the spare keys.

I drove straight to the hospital and we got there the same time as Lucy was walking out. Just the way she looked as she walked towards us told us everything.

'There was nothing the doctors could have done,' she said. 'Mum had a massive heart attack.'

Mum had died in my arms as I placed her into the car. It was no comfort because my own heart was absolutely shattered.

We buried Mum in Pinjarra, the ancestral home of her beloved Binjarib people. It gave us some comfort to know our mum's spirit was in a safe place with her people. As a family, we had to take extra care of Dad after Mum passed away. He was absolutely heartbroken and felt so lost without Mum. She was the love of his life, his mate, the mother of his kids, his everything.

Over the following months, at his lowest points, Dad often said he wanted to join her in death. Every one of us rallied around Dad and kept him going, but losing Mum was tough on all of us for a long, long time.

And not just for us, it was also devastating for her siblings, in-laws and their families. Our mum was so special and meant so much to a lot of people, black and white fullas included. Dad received cards and kind words from everyone, including the wadjerlars. All those wadjerlar families Mum had worked for as a housekeeper and cook were especially affected. She had worked for them for such a long time they had often told her she was part of their family. The shopkeepers where Mum and Dad had credit expressed their sympathy to all our family. It was like everyone in our small town felt her passing.

I missed my mum terribly. The need to care for my children was the one thing that got me through. I knew Mum would never want me to neglect them. So in honour of my mum, and what she had taught us throughout her life, I focused all my energy and time on being the best mum I could to my little family.

CAUGHT OUT

It was the end of the week and I had just put the three big kids off to school and settled the two younger ones in front of the television. Jason and Tedo had gone to work an hour earlier, so I had the house to myself. Being Friday, I put a wash in the machine just in case we went somewhere special on the weekend. I was in the midst of cleaning up after breakfast because Lucy was due any minute to see the two little ones for their health check-ups.

Since Mum had passed away three months before, Lucy had been checking in nearly every day to see if we were okay. I think it helped her as well because she was also having to cope with losing Mum. Soon enough, the little Community Health car pulled up in the driveway. I put the kettle on and set up the mugs for our tea. I was looking forward to catching up on the latest local Nyoongar gossip. Lucy never disclosed any information about her clients' health, but we did yarn about everything else going on in our community.

Rummaging around for some biscuits, I was surprised that Lucy hadn't gotten out of the car yet. When I looked out the window, she was still sitting there. So I walked out to the front verandah and waved her to come in, signalling our cuppa was ready in the kitchen.

But as she got out I could see there was something weighing on her mind. Instead of coming inside, she sat on the top step of the verandah. She asked quietly, 'Do you mind if we had a yarn first?'

I told her we could have our tea outside, but she shook her head and said, 'Not just yet'. Then she blurted it out: 'There's no easy way to tell you, sis. You remember telling me last Monday morning that Jason told you he would be playing darts and would stay at his mate's place on Monday night? To save you picking him up so late?'

I nodded.

'Well, I had a very early appointment in Mandurah on Tuesday and I picked the car up at six in the morning. I had my bloke in the car with me at the time. On our way to Mandurah, at the Yunderup turn-off we saw Dot's green car turning right, heading towards Pinjarra. The only two people in the car were her and Jason. Jono wasn't there. I'm sorry I had to tell you this. But I couldn't live with myself, letting you be made a fool of by those two.' She was nearly in tears as she continued. 'My bloke told me to keep it to myself, that it is none of my business. We been arguing every day since we saw them two. Arguing about what I should do. But you're my sister, Lavinia. I had to let you know. I have been asking around and apparently they've been running each other for a long while now. Even before you left Medina.'

I didn't want to believe Lucy, but her face told me she was telling the truth. All this time my husband had been sneaking around with my brother's wife. It seemed everyone in our small town knew about it except me. Me, the good wife. Me, the utter fool. Too busy doing the right thing by him and our children.

Lucy and I never did have that cup of tea. Both of us were too upset. After checking I would be okay, Lucy left to go back to work. I walked inside, plonked myself on the nearest lounge chair and sat there blankly staring. My thoughts were in turmoil. I blamed myself for being so dumb, so blind, so stupid and so trusting.

I wondered why I had not seen something sooner. Why had I not put the pieces together and realised all the times Dot kept coming around to our place, first in Medina and later after we moved back to Pinjarra, she was coming to see Jason? She would turn up drunk at the old place with other people, and leave after Jason went out and spoke with them. And that was after Dad threatened to put the police on her for disturbing us at one o'clock in the morning.

It must have been two hours later, when I had to give Shane his heart medicine and make lunch for him and Gary that I actually started to feel something return to normal. Thank God for children.

The showdown came as soon as Jason got home from work. I confronted him with what I had heard and of course he denied it. Mind you, he didn't call Lucy an outright liar. We couldn't really get into it because his white mates pulled up. It was their darts grand final and they had to play first up. He said he would be back as soon as the game was over.

Surprisingly true to his word, Jason came home straight after darts, trophy in hand. Our kids and all the others who lived in the house were happy for him. He shared a few beers with his dad, his sister and his brother-in-law to celebrate. Their happy mood prevailed so nothing could really be sorted out between us. After giving Shane his midnight medicine, I went to sleep. The day had been long and fraught with stress and unanswered questions, and I was exhausted. I forced myself to let it go for now. I desperately needed a rest. I grabbed a pillow and some blankets and slept on the couch in the lounge.

I must have woken up at about 7.30 am. The kids were already up and watching Saturday morning cartoons. As I made my cuppa, they reminded me of my promise to take them to the local community fair that day. I couldn't see Jason anywhere and when I asked them where he was, they said he had been picked up earlier, about an hour ago.

'What? Who picked him up?'

I already knew the answer. Still, the kids told me that Jason's niece had come to the door and got him. She told them they were going over to the reserve. Then they had taken off in Dot's car.

A deep anger welled up inside me. But just as soon as it came, I quashed it. Instead, as though by instinct, I knew what I had to do. I had a wash, got dressed, tied my hair up and walked out the door. I told my kids to wait at the house.

I grabbed a koondee the size of a four-by-two, and went looking for them. I was cutting across the vacant block, big stick in hand, when I saw Jason coming towards me. He saw me, but instead of meeting me he walked right around, not coming within fifty metres of me. He had seen the stick I was holding and was giving me a wide berth. I yelled to him, 'I'll be back for you when I finish with your slut. I promise you that, you lying, sneaking prick.' He wouldn't come near me.

When I got to the reserve, I could see Dot sitting on the bonnet of her car, beer bottle in hand. They were at Jason's cousin's house and there were a few other people drinking with her. They suddenly went silent. She saw me coming, but in all her arrogance just started laughing right at me. Without saying a word, I walked straight up to her and knocked the beer bottle out of her hand with the stick. Beer bottle and stick both went flying. I grabbed her by the hair and dragged her down off the bonnet, punching her in the face all the way down. Once she hit the ground, I straddled her and kept punching with both fists. She tried to hit me back, but her arms were too short and I had no trouble pounding her face and head with both fists. My anger was focused totally on Dot and she got the full force of it.

I could vaguely hear people screaming and shouting in the background. One woman was screaming, 'Stop, you gunna kill her, Lavinia. For fuck's sake, stop!'

I felt a thud to my right temple, and I then was dragged off Dot.

Once upright, I turned and started kicking her in the head and body. Someone pushed me over and I rolled away, putting distance between me and whoever it was. I jumped up to face the person, ready to defend myself.

Only some men stood there. Dot was lying on the ground. The men had formed a barrier between us two women. One of them tried to lift her up. When he couldn't, another person came to help and they dragged her away into the house.

I stood there for a minute. Nothing. No threat. Apart from stopping me from doing her any more harm, not one of them said or did anything. I grabbed my stick and walked back to my house. Their father was nowhere in sight. Even though he had a big reputation for beating every man who had ever challenged him for a fight, he didn't come anywhere near me. That day I learned that an angry woman with a big koondee can scare even the bravest of cheating pricks.

A couple of hours later, on my way to take the kids to the fair, I was stopped by the local police. Constable Jewel told me to go by the police station. Apparently, the sergeant wanted to talk to me about a woman who claimed I had assaulted her. So I pushed the pram with Shane, Gary and Alison on board, and with my two older boys walking alongside me, we went to the police station. Of course, Dot was there.

I felt nothing inside when I saw that slut with the two puffed up black eyes, the smashed and swollen mouth and the broken nose I had given her. She started screaming and swearing at me, but she didn't make a move towards where I stood. I made sure I stayed between her and my kids. When the sergeant questioned me I calmly told him and Constable Jewel that I had nothing to do with her injuries, that she must have gotten me mixed up with somebody else. The police said they couldn't get anyone on the reserve to talk about it. Not one witness. Nyoongar silence? Nyoongar justice, maybe.

The police told me I could go about my business. It was only then that I allowed myself to feel something. It was absolute and total disgust towards her. Disgust and betrayal. She was my brother's wife, mother of his four kids. She'd been in our family for so many years. For goodness sake, I had been a bridesmaid when she married Jono.

Something in me died that day as I walked out of the police station, listening to her still swearing, cursing and making threats at me. In its place was a quite resolve to leave all this shit behind me. Surely there had to be something better in this world for me and my kids.

At twenty-five, I was still pretty young. I had led a respectable, church-going life caring for my family as I had been taught by my mum and my mum-in-law. I had to help myself and my children. It wasn't going to be easy, I knew that for sure. I realised that I had to change my mindset. In that instant, I grew up.

A DOWNWARD SPIRAL

When my sister Verna drove down later that day to pick me and my kids up, I had two small cases already packed. I had already taken Gary over to his nanna's place with all his clothes and explained that I was leaving. I think she had already heard about, and may have witnessed, what had happened at the reserve. She wasn't surprised at all when I took Gary to her place. I told her I couldn't take him with me; I didn't have much money and now me and my four kids didn't have a roof over our heads either. At least Gary would be with his family. I didn't know where we would go or what our future held. I just had to get away.

Aside from a few photos of my kids and some important papers, everything else I had collected and treasured over the years was left behind. Just like my naivety, my youth and my trust in others. They no longer existed. There was nothing there for me anymore.

I was thankful that Verna let me stay with her. It was a tight squeeze in her four-bedroom state house, me and my four kids, Verna and her six. Twelve people in a four-bedroom state house. Then there was the possibility that her husband, from whom she was separated, might return. He had a very mean disposition and nobody wanted to be around him for any length of time.

I had been a week at Verna's place in South Perth, just trying to work my way through all that had happened, when I realised I still I had to go back and collect some other important papers from

Pinjarra. Verna had a bit of time off work and took me down there. After asking if I would be alright, she dropped me in town, then went on to visit her friends, promising to pick me up in an hour.

Being back in Pinjarra, even for an hour, was an ordeal. It reminded me of the day Lucy first told me about catching Jason and Dot together. I hadn't had any contact with Jason since I went to Verna's place. I was still angry and I wasn't sure what I would have done if I had seen him.

All the questions came flooding back. Why hadn't I noticed what was happening? How come all those people knew about them and not one person had the decency to tell me? They were supposed to be my friends, my relatives. Thank God Lucy told me, even though she knew it would hurt me. Tears began to flow and my body felt racked with deep pain, but I told myself that I had to survive and look after my four children. They needed me. I had to be okay.

It's funny how pain and hurt can manifest itself. The final bit of business I had to do that day was to go to the local post office in Pinjarra to redirect my mail to Verna's place. As I was leaving the building, my arms and legs refused to move. It was as if they were weighted down with lead. Then they shut down. I crumbled onto the post office steps.

My friend Isla, who was headed into the post office on her own business, rushed over to help me. She put her arms around me and tried to help me up. It wasn't happening. I was ten kilos lighter than her, but she could not lift me. And I couldn't hold my own weight. My arms and legs felt like rubber. Confused and upset, Isla screamed for help from passers-by and sat there holding me, tears streaming down both our faces, waiting for the ambulance. I think she thought I was going to die right then and there. I was taken to the local hospital by ambulance. Verna found me there and spoke at length with the doctors.

After many tests, the doctors could find nothing physically wrong with me. They told Verna the problem must be psychological. Whatever it was, it frightened me properly. I was kept in hospital for two days. During that time, the doctor gave me medication to help me sleep. He said I needed to rest. The medicine must have given my troubled mind some respite from the fucked-up way I had been treated by people I regarded as my family and friends.

For the first time in weeks, I slept soundly. The next day I seemed a bit better. The day after that I was strong enough to get out of hospital. My mind and spirit were bruised, but at least my body was functioning.

My friend Isla came to visit me and, despite my protests, gave me some money. She then helped me to contact Verna to let her know I was being discharged. When I left, the doctor did say I might have a relapse. I didn't ever want that to happen again. Being immobile, even temporarily, is terrible. As I walked out of hospital that morning, I made a conscious decision to get on with my life. I still had myself and my four young children to look after.

I was later told, when I gave little Gary back to his family, it broke his heart. Separating from him compounded my pain and that of my children. I had been caring for the little boy since he was only four months old. He was nearly three years old when we left and I knew he didn't understand what was happening. But he was with people who loved him and I knew he would be safe.

The home we had in Pinjarra was no longer there for us. I had been a part of the Kagan family since I was fifteen. A full decade. I had shared their good times and bad. They had shared in mine too. Now it was all over.

Of course I couldn't go and stay with my brother Jono – Dot's husband – since I had flogged his wife. Jono had four kids to raise too and he had to deal with a wife who had been running around behind his back for God knows how long, with a bloke who had been his friend since childhood.

Sometimes gut-wrenching pain can be a blessing. Even if you don't recognise it when you are hurting. During that time, I changed. To stop me going kaartwarra and to get through each day, I would think about what my mum had said if things ever got me down.

'Lavinia, always look for at least one thing that is good about the day God has given us. It might be the sunshine, a flower, a smile or even a little child. One positive aspect. Something that gives you a reason to show that it is worthwhile to be alive.'

For me, that reason was my children. I knew I had to be strong for them, but it was very hard. There were times when I would just break down and cry, overwhelmed by emotion and sadness. I was not sure what direction our lives were going to take. But I have found that in times of crisis, sheer determination and anger can save your life

SMALL CONSOLATION

We found out a couple of months later how Jono felt about the situation. Verna came home and told me that our brother had waited in the bushes and hit Jason on the head with a big rock. That had happened one night in Medina. Jono had rung Verna to tell her he didn't know whether he had killed Jason or not. He didn't care. He had just left him there for dead.

I got on the phone and asked Jono if he confronted Dot about what they had done, and were still doing. He said she was not to blame. I could not believe my ears! Every second day or so, she had driven down to wherever we were staying and sought out Jason. Not that I was excusing Jason in any way either. It takes two to tango.

I contacted a cousin in Medina and asked if she had heard anything on the Nyoongar grapevine about the beating. She told me Jason was in hospital in Fremantle. He had been taken there by ambulance with severe damage to his head. Yes, he had been attacked, but no, he didn't see who had hit him with the big rock. The police were looking into it, but didn't have anything to go on.

I didn't pursue the issue. And Jason was no longer my concern. He had chosen that woman over our family. Let him live with it. I already had enough on my plate to worry about. Besides, we hadn't heard from him for months.

When we were living at Verna's, I didn't have a car, so we caught buses whenever we had to go to doctor appointments right in the city. Shane still needed round-the-clock medication and it was crucial we kept his appointments with heart specialists. I was grateful for the few times Verna took us to those appointments in her car.

That was whenever she could because she was working full-time. Also, she had her own schedules to keep and her own young ones to raise. Her daughter Aarlia was company for me and she was a big help by just being there.

Of course, State Housing got wind of the overcrowding situation at Verna's and said I had to move out with my kids or Verna would lose her house. That put me in another spin. To top it off, Child Welfare got in on the act. They threatened to take my children from me if I didn't have a home of my own. I still had the debt from the house in Medina, so getting a state housing place was a real long shot. Verna wrote to State Housing, advising them of my situation, and asked that we be given time to find alternative accommodation. Thankfully, we were given permission to stay at her place for another two months. After that, we were homeless.

My health was also still at risk. I had lost so much weight and looked downright haggard. I wasn't playing sport anymore. I couldn't sleep, but I had to keep going for my kids' sake. The stress of everything that had happened, and was still happening, was taking its toll on me.

An ordinary bout of the flu turned into pneumonia. I was given antibiotics and told to rest or I would be hospitalised. Then Child Welfare got wind that I was sick. Back then, in 1976, being a Nyoongar and still under government policy, it wasn't unusual for government departments to share personal information about clients between agencies. We belonged to the state and I was just another number.

I got a visit from one Child Welfare officer who said if I wasn't healthy enough to take care of my kids, they would take them from me until the kids turned eighteen. Another kick in the guts. However, that welfare officer did give me a choice.

If I agreed to them taking my children while I was ill, then when I got better, I could take them out myself. No court case. But of course, when I did eventually get a home for us, it still had to be approved by Child Welfare officers.

My kids and I were on their books and, like so many other government agencies supposedly looking after us poor black people, I was an example that justified their department's existence. They had to do what they deemed best for us. For our own good they said.

I couldn't see how breaking up an already broken family could possibly help me and my kids. But what choice did I have? With Verna's support it was organised that my four little ones would be taken to Roelands Mission, 170 kilometres south of Perth, to be cared for by foster parents. The mission was now being run by the Baptist church. Verna's children had previously spent some time in the same place and they said it was pretty good.

With a heavy heart, I went down with Verna to drop off my kids. Jason Junior and Aimon would be housed in a building with older kids and cared for by a married couple. Shane and Ali would be cared for in a cottage by a young single woman named Lana. I was assured that Shane would be cared for and that his appointments with the heart specialists would be kept. It was agreed that Lana and I would go together to those appointments. I wanted to make sure everything was alright with my baby and his still very serious heart condition.

The manager of the mission was a Mr Buttley. It was agreed that they would take four-fifths of my income to pay for my children's costs while in foster care. It didn't leave me with much money, but at least I could get my little ones out without too much trouble and red tape when the time came.

At least the older kids thought moving into the mission as an adventure, but it was a devastating time for me. I had done nothing wrong, yet here I was about to leave them with strangers. It made me feel as if my whole life was coming to an end.

On the way back to Verna's, I didn't stop crying until we got to Waroona, some sixty kilometres north of Roelands. Verna drove and I cried – at first, big broken-hearted sobs, then the deep, silent pain accompanied by a steady flow of tears that just wouldn't stop.

A NEW DIRECTION

My physical and emotional health took forever to improve. Verna concentrated on getting vitamin supplements and nourishing food into me and helping me keep my doctor appointments. My niece Aarlia was a really good cook and she got me to help by peeling all the vegies she needed. Today it is usually called occupational therapy. Whatever they called it back then, being useful helped and slowly I improved.

Over the next few months, on the week that I got paid from Social Services, I went to Roelands Mission to see my children. I caught the *Australind* train to Brunswick Junction, which took an hour and a half travel. Lana would pick me up and drive me to the mission. I spent about five hours with my children, then I was dropped back at Brunswick to catch the train to Perth. From there I got the bus back to Verna's place in South Perth. The visits took almost a full day. At first, it knocked me for six. But getting to see them, even for those few hours each time, I steadily began to heal. It also helped the kids to see me and it helped them to understand I had not abandoned them.

After my children were taken, and as I grew better, I began to apply for jobs and courses. My employment skills and experience were not great. I had been a casual housemaid and babysitter in Pinjarra, then had the job with the Roussells in Wanneroo, and

I had worked for the florist in Perth. Since having babies at sixteen, I had not worked in paid employment.

One day about six months later, I saw a notice in the paper calling for Aboriginal people to enrol to do a teachers training course at Mount Lawley Teachers College – now known as Edith Cowan University. With some trepidation, I applied but I didn't really trust my chances of getting accepted. I had only gone to Year 10, but my marks back then were pretty good. But to get into university level? Regardless, I posted the application and I left it at that.

A few weeks later I had a visit from Leira and my brother-in-law Tedo. The three of us hadn't talked much about Jason and Dot and what had happened. There was no need for it. Those two had been a part of my life since we were all kids. As children, I considered Leira my best friend and as adults that had not changed. And she too had been affected badly by the events of the past year.

When they turned up to see how I was doing, we swapped yarns, then they asked if I would like to play basketball again for the Pinjarra Wildcats Women. There was a new competition starting up, plus a few carnivals were happening in the next couple of months.

They said they would pick me up next week. Just for a look – no rush. I agreed to come and have a look, but I told them there had to be room for two people because I wasn't going anywhere without Aarlia. My niece had become my friend, confidante and someone who kept me grounded when I needed it most.

Around the same time, I found out the application I sent in to attend teacher training was being considered by the panel overseeing the program. I had to go sit an aptitude test to see if I could get one of the ten or so placements on offer. Verna and Aarlia were very encouraging and supportive because they knew my morale was still very low.

Without too many expectations, I attended the testing. Lo and behold, I was accepted into the course! I had to start attending classes and studying within the next month, and they would pay me to study! Being accepted and starting those studies would prove to have a huge impact in saving my sanity and my ego.

Training to be a teacher turned out to be a steep learning curve. I knew nothing about tertiary education. But I wanted to learn and I was determined to do so. I caught buses from Verna's place and had to walk a few kilometres every day, but I attended classes and did my assignments.

I made some new friends, even though I was a bit older than most of the students in our first-year group, which was made up of both young women and young men. I was nearly twenty-six years old and some of them, at eighteen, were straight out of high school. These Aboriginal teenagers had more academic knowledge about assignments, but I had more life experience. Still, we all got on really well and supported each other. They told us at the time that this teacher-training program was the first of its kind in Western Australia, maybe the whole country. We felt a bit like guinea pigs, but it was accompanied by the excitement of the challenge that us black students could actually do it.

I could feel myself getting stronger as the weeks of study and learning turned into months. It was a bit of a struggle, but I managed to complete the first year. My finances improved as well because I was getting paid to study. Before that, four-fifths of my income was being channelled by Native Welfare straight to Roelands Mission. What little money I did get was spent on board to Verna and bus and train fares.

For my children and me, that first year was the hardest of our lives. Jason Junior and Aimon were struggling with the situation, often getting into trouble with Mr Buttley.

Somewhere during that time, I found out they were getting punished for their perceived misbehaviour and I made a concerted effort to get them out of the mission as soon as possible. I set about saving money to buy a car and get a deposit to rent a house of our own. I also put in another application for State Housing assistance. This time for only me and the children.

I managed to complete my first year of the teaching course with good results. Into the second year, with a new intake of students, Leira started the teacher training too. Because she was listed as a 'country student', she was given accommodation assistance and housing support in the metro area close to the college.

Around the same time, I received news that Shane was to have open heart surgery to fix the hole in his koort. When I got the news, I said extra prayers to God every day for strength for us all to get through it.

Before Shane's heart operation, I had to meet with social workers and speak to doctors from the hospital. They told me there were some important papers that had to be signed by both parents. The hospital made it very clear that Shane's operation couldn't happen without Jason's signature. They went to great lengths and explained that both parents had to approve. If one didn't agree and it went ahead, the hospital could face legal issues. It meant I had to make contact with Jason. When I asked what she thought, Verna said to take Aarlia, Leira or someone else with me on the day – just in case things turned out badly.

So with Aarlia in tow, I went down to Medina to tell Jason that he had to make himself available to sign those papers and attend a family information appointment with the doctor performing the procedure.

Feeling apprehensive but determined, I went to Medina. I was shocked at Jason's appearance. He looked horrible. Hungover and skinny. Like he had been hitting the booze full-on and not eating. Still, I reminded myself, it was his choice. None of my business.

Through the Nyoongar grapevine I had heard many rumours. Even if I wasn't interested, it seemed people still made a point of telling me what Jason was up to. Nyoongar gossipers told me that he was still running around with Dot. In fact, Jason and Dot were living together at his cousin's place in Medina. I had heard that she *was still living part of the time* at her home with Jono, then going back to be with Jason.

The day I spoke with Jason about the need to sign papers for Shane's impending heart operation, Dot was not there. His cousins were teasing him, saying they were going to tell Dot about him talking to me. The drunken idiots were laughing, saying Jason would be in the shit with her when she found out I had been to see him.

I passed on the news as a legal requirement and gave him the address and dates of when and where we had to meet with the hospital's medical team to sign papers. I now had his cousin's address in Medina and I could send any other information to him through the post. Whether he would receive any mail I might send was doubtful because the people he lived with were unreliable alcoholics. Like so many of us Nyoongars, letters had very little importance to them.

Jason asked me about our koolungahs, but I just shrugged. I got the feeling that he wanted to talk with me some more, but I was having none of that bullshit. After saying Shane's operation would take place in about three months, I got out of there without so much as a see ya later.

One thing I did know was I had no feelings left for him. There was no anger, no spite and definitely no love. Sure, he was my kids' father, and I made a point of never rubbishing him in front of them, but he was nothing to me. Some hurt and humiliation go a bit too deep.

The very next week, Jason rang Verna at work to pass on a message to me. He wanted to go down and see his children. Especially Shane. That threw me. For the first time in two years he wanted to see his kids. I doubt he ever really loved me or wanted to be settled down with me in the first place. Fathering the kids didn't change that and I figured because they were a part of me, he didn't want to be around them either. And even when we were a family all living together, Jason was rarely there to care for me or his kids.

I don't know what caused his change of heart now. Maybe he'd grown up. The very next week, Leira drove him down there to visit the kids. I was already there at the time when they turned up. At least he looked a bit better than when I had last seen him in Medina. He'd had a shave and had clean clothes on, but he still looked very skinny and gaunt.

Things were strained between us that day at Roelands. I had nothing to say to him. I was glad that Leira had driven him down to see the koolungáhs because it gave me a chance to catch up with her for a yarn away from teachers college and basketball. Leira and Jason stayed quite a while with the little ones, but left a couple of hours before me. I could tell the kids were very happy to see their dad, though it took a while for them to warm up to him.

MOORDITJ KOORT

The day of Shane's operation rolled around. In order to ease my mind in the lead-up to the procedure, I fired endless questions at Verna, who was a fully qualified nurse. And I also read every bit of information I could about heart operations. The doctors and nursing staff at the hospital were very good at answering my questions as well. They said the heart surgeon who was heading the operation had travelled across from Sydney. His name was Dr Chang and he had an excellent track record. He was a leader in his field. Still, I was very worried because Shane was only five years old and looked so very small and vulnerable as they wheeled him into the operating theatre.

I was also very grateful that Aarlia had come to keep me company. Leira had brought Jason up to the hospital as well, and the four of us sat in the waiting room. I had never felt so helpless. My baby's life was out of my hands and I had no option but to leave it up to God and the doctors to make him well.

It was the longest five hours I have ever spent. After an hour, Leira went out to get a feed and Jason went out to have a smoke. He stayed outside for the longest time and Leira told me he had felt so sick he had vomited. I knew he couldn't stand being in a hospital for too long, so I wasn't surprised. I remembered his mum telling me he had been born in a tent and that, for some reason, he couldn't stand being in any hospital. She thought it was the smell of the place that made him ill. But it also crossed my mind that he had hardly ever been there when we needed him, so what else was new.

Jason ended up waiting in the church grounds opposite the hospital. I left it to Leira to race out and get him when the nurse told us that the heart surgeon would be coming to talk to us soon. Holding on tightly to Aarlia's hand, I was on the verge of tears. In silence and with grave faces, the four of us waited for the doctor.

Suddenly, a diminutive man walked through the door and introduced himself to us as Dr Chang. He told us the operation had been a total success and we would be allowed to see Shane soon. I felt so relieved that I actually looked at the ceiling and thanked the Lord out loud. I also said a silent thank you to the old spirits who I knew were looking after Shane. I then thanked Dr Chang and shook his hand. We were so happy, our faces were beaming. About half an hour later, a nurse came and asked if we wanted to see the patient, but only two at a time. Jason and I went in first.

It was terribly confronting. Super bright lights overhead, beeping machines monitoring everything, tubes and bandages everywhere, and the strong smell of anesthetic seemed overwhelming. Two nurses were in constant attendance checking everything.

Right there in the middle of all that medical paraphernalia was Shane. Although groggy, my baby boy was awake and complaining, 'I hate these nurses, Mum. I am so hungry and they won't even feed me anything.'

I explained to him very gently it was the doctors who decided when he would be allowed to eat.

His comeback was, 'Then I hate the doctors too.' His grumpy, groggy words were the sweetest music I have ever heard. I knew then he was going to be fine. I gave him a kiss on his little forehead and Jason did the same. Shane then dozed off.

We grabbed a chair each and sat on either side of the bed, holding his chubby little brown hands. Again I silently thanked God for His mercy and the success of the heart operation. While we waited for Shane to come around properly, I kept looking from his beautiful little face to the monitors and back. Checking and double-checking that everything was still working right.

Then, a side movement caught my eye. I looked across Shane's bed at Jason. He was swaying and had turned a very pale grey. I pressed the button to call the nurses who had only just stepped out.

They rushed back in and looked straight toward Shane and the machines, but I pointed to Jason. He was clinging to the base of the bed and by now threatening to throw up as well. One of the nurses *helped him to his feet and quickly led him out of the operation* recovery theatre. It was wicked of me I know, but I nearly started laughing.

The nurse came back and asked if I was okay. No worries for me. I sat with Shane for about an hour during which time both Leira and Aarlia each took a turn to look in on us. I never left my baby boy's side. I passed on his message about wanting some food to the nurses. They said he would be fed something very light the next morning. And they seemed impressed with his cheeky words. It showed them that he had lively spirit and was making real progress.

Knowing Shane was recovering well from his surgery, and on the doctor's advice, we left after about four hours. Before I walked out of the waiting room, Dr Chang gave me a small plastic jar. He said it contained the wires that had kept Shane alive during the operation. He explained they actually took his heart right out of his chest to stitch up the hole in his little heart. Dr Chang's team then put Shane's heart back inside his chest and closed the massive hole in his chest. Those few wires kept everything else on track.

I gratefully accepted the small plastic jar and vowed that I would hold on to those wires forever. I don't know if God ever gets tired of us saying thank you, but that day he must have heard me saying it a million times.

Shane stayed in hospital for nearly a month. Leira, who was living in a private house not far from the teachers college asked if I wanted to move in with her. I could bring Shane to live with us as well when he got released. I agreed because I hated the idea of Shane going back down to Roelands Mission.

The time I spent in the recovery ward with Shane, watching him get stronger every day, was worth every minute of the pain and suffering I had been through. Having my baby son with me made me realise I wanted all my children back with me. I was feeling so much healthier and stronger. Well enough to care for them. After a fortnight of finalising everything, I arranged for my other three kids to live with me at Leira's place. Her house was not a state house and I was thankful that I had made that agreement with the child welfare officer where I could collect my children whenever I was ready to. I was so glad that I was able to take them out of the mission without interference from any government agency.

After my kids and I had moved in with Leira, Jason would often come and visit them. We had gotten back to talking and one day, he told me and Leira that he and Dot were though. They had parted a few months ago.

To my surprise, not long after that, he asked if we could get back together and live as a family. He said he wanted to be with me and our children. I still had doubts and I sought advice from Leira. She reminded me that before anything else, we must consider the kids and what they had gone through.

I thought long and hard about what I should do. It had been going on four years since Jason and I had separated. One good thing was, whatever our future held I knew that my kids and I would survive with or without him in our lives. I had no guarantee about how long it would last this time, but was I willing to at least give it a go for our children.

TIME TO HEAL

We were at Leira's place for six months when, quite unexpectedly, I was sent a letter from State Housing. I had all but given up hope, but after four years of being on the original waiting list, and paying off my state housing debt, a place had become available for us in Pinjarra. I don't know if anybody had pulled any strings or the timing was just a coincidence, but I didn't question it. All that was needed was a small deposit and to sign the papers.

We moved into a four-bedroom house and slowly got enough furniture to make it into a home. Things had definitely changed for all of us. The kids were older and so much more self-sufficient. Following his successful heart operation, Shane no longer needed round-the-clock medication. The biggest change though was that I had grown into a strong Nyoongar woman. Within myself I felt a very strong emotional, spiritual and psychological inner strength that was not there before. It was something Jason recognised as well. I was never going to take any shit from him or anyone else ever again. He took to being home with me and the kids more than ever before.

We all got into local sports with the boys playing basketball and football. I played netball and basketball and Jason got into footy and darts. He only went to the pub for darts on the Friday evening and was back home by nine o'clock at the latest. The biggest change I noticed was if he wanted a beer, he would bring a few back home.

It never happened very often, but whenever it did, he would sit around a fire in the backyard playing the guitar and yarning with Tony, my nephew.

Like me, Tony's wife, Lola, didn't drink alcohol, and the four of us got on really well. They ended up moving in with us while they waited for their own place to come through from State Housing. For the first time ever, as a family unit we went on trips with Jason's brother Tedo, his wife Gwenda, and their little family. On those outings, Jason's dad, Old Ted, also came along with Leira and her boys in company with Patty and Marty and their youngest son. It was quality family time and a lot of laughter and fun.

Jason found a good job working for a building company as a labourer. Although I had put my teaching degree on hold, I took to tutoring other Nyoongar people in town who were studying to further their education. We were kept pretty busy with the kids all in school now. On the weekends, when we had the money, we would go out with other family members for picnics, to the river fishing and swimming or to the estuary for crabbing. It was good to see Jason and his three sons doing things together. He was also spending more time with Old Ted. Maybe Jason had grown up too and was finally learning how to be a good family man.

We must have been back together for about six months when Dot reappeared in the picture. I heard she had driven down to Pinjarra a few times over the preceding weeks. Rumours got around that she wanted to pick up with Jason again.

One Friday evening, a darts night, Jason came home very early. The kids and I were still up watching television. Something was bothering him. I got up and walked into the kitchen indicating for him to follow me. I switched the kettle on then walked out the back door. Once outside, even before I asked him anything, he told me straight out. Dot had been drinking and she had gone down to the pub and asked him to go with her again. When he refused and walked away from her, she swore him upside down. Right there in the pub, in front of everyone, she threatened to kill him. He left his mates at the dart competition and walked out of the pub.

Still agitated, as we walked back into the kitchen he said to me, 'Lavinia, I don't want anything to do with Dot. Why don't you go and tell her to fuck off and leave me alone.'

I turned and looked him straight in the eye. I shook my head. Very slowly and deliberately, without any emotion, I said, 'No Jason, you got involved with her in the first place. You invited her into our marriage. Grab some balls and you tell her yourself to fuck off and leave *you* alone. You do it! And when you say it, mean it. I'm not fighting or arguing with any moll for you ever again. I don't care one way or another. You of all people know that the kids and I can survive without you. We can and will live without you. It's your choice now. But if you go with her, don't ever look to come back to us. You choose.' I didn't bother with making a cuppa. I turned and walked back into the lounge, sat down and continued watching television.

The next afternoon my nephew and Jason went over to his brother's place. They were working on their mate's car, which was parked in Tedo's driveway. Without any warning, Dot turned up.

Gwenda filled me in on the rest of what happened. She said Dot asked Jason in front of everyone there why he hadn't gone with her last night. For a few minutes, there was silence. Again, Dot demanded to know why Jason hadn't gone with her.

His response, when he finally spoke up, was very loud. He started by shouting at her to fuck right off. To fuck off and leave him alone. He called her a black cunt. Told her he didn't want anything to do with her ever again and to get out of his face and out of his life. For good!

Gwenda told me, 'Jason said straight out he wanted to be with you, Lavinia, and you fullas' kids. When he mentioned your name, Dot went right off her head.'

Gwenda went on to say no one expected what happened next. Jason was standing in the driveway and Dot started her car and drove straight at him. Jason jumped out of the way onto the grass. She backed up, then revved the engine up again. The car easily mounted the small kerb onto the grass and came straight for him.

Again he sprang out of the way just in time, the wheels barely missing him. Everyone was screaming and shouting at her to stop, but she wouldn't.

Jason's cousin saw what was happening and knew that she was not going to stop. He picked up a huge garden rock and threw it right through the front windscreen of Dot's car, smashing it. With the rock on the front seat and glass fragments everywhere, it made her slam on the brakes. Gwenda said Dot immediately put the car in reverse and backed out of the place. Madly spinning the wheels, causing black smoke to rise from the bitumen road, she took off down the street, screaming and swearing all the way.

Gwenda told me the police came by soon after, trying to get information about who broke the front window of Dot's car. Dot had put a report in to the police and wanted to press charges against the rock thrower. As usual within our Nyoongar community, nobody saw who threw the rock, so police couldn't help her. And it was clear that Dot never mentioned to the police about her trying to kill Jason with her car in the first place.

After a while, Jason himself got around to telling me what happened at Tedo and Gwenda's house that day. I said he should report her to the police for trying to kill him with her car. But Jason reckoned if he did that, he would have to see the bitch again in court. Enough was enough. He wanted us to move on.

People hardly saw anything of Dot in Pinjarra after that incident. There was the one time at a funeral some six months later when she came down with Jono and their children. She looked heavily pregnant, so maybe she and Jono had moved on too. They didn't stay long and went back home straight after the burial.

Another time she was seen was when she came to pick up her brother George who had gotten stranded down in Pinjarra. The message must have finally gotten through to her brain that it was finally over between her and Jason.

TRAGEDY

One day I came home to find Jason standing in the backyard. I had been doing some shopping for the kids' lunch. It was a bit surprising because usually he was away from seven in the morning until five o'clock in the evening. Instead of going through the front door, I walked around the house to join him. When he sat down on the back stairs, I asked him to move over so I could sit next to him. He told me he had been working just around the corner so had made his way home for lunch.

I was puzzled why he wasn't inside making a cuppa. We had our front door key which was attached to the car keys, but we didn't have one for the back door. Whenever we all left the house, we took to slotting a knife across the back door to keep it locked. To get it open all that was needed was a slight push and the knife would fall. I wondered why Jason hadn't just pushed on the back door. He told me he had tried that, but still couldn't open it. I got up and gave the back door a slight push. I heard the knife fall as usual and after opening the door, we went inside. While we were having lunch, Jason said he felt a bit of a headache. I wanted him to tell his boss he was taking the rest of the day off. However, he went back to work after taking some Bex powders, the favourite headache cure for us Nyoongars.

Early the next day, Jason again complained of not feeling well. He mentioned painful headaches and weakness in his upper body.

He surmised he must have lifted something too heavy while on the job. I insisted he go to the doctor for a check-up. His response was to take some more Bex and head to work.

Feeling worried, I made an appointment with the doctor for him. I also went over to talk with Leira, Old Ted, Tedo and Gwenda about it. We all knew Jason was stubborn about seeing doctors and more so about going to hospital. His crew was working nearby, so when Jason came home for lunch, the four of us talked him into seeing the doctor after work that day.

He complained that we were all trying to bully him, but finally agreed that he needed to get medical advice. So he kept the appointment and all sorts of tests were taken and sent to Perth. The doctor then made another booking to see Jason the following Thursday when his test results would be back. In the meantime, he was not allowed to return to work.

At that time, medical technology was okay, but not as precise as it is now. The results came back on Thursday showing nothing too unusual, so the doctor gave Jason a prescription for strong painkillers and a week off work with total rest. Definitely no lifting anything heavier than a cup of tea was his instruction to Jason.

Come Friday, I woke with a sick feeling. I couldn't understand what it was, but I got the kids their breakfast and then took them to school. I had to drop our car off at Tedo and Gwenda's place for some repairs and walk the short distance back to our house. When I got back home Jason, my nephew Tony and his wife, Lola, were having a final cuppa and starting to clean up. I did some washing and around twelve I joined them three watching the midday movie on television. Winter was making itself felt and the wind had an icy sting to it so we were all happy to stay in the warm.

That afternoon Tony and Lola had plans to go away for the weekend so they started packing some things. After the kids got home from school, Tony got news their ride couldn't make it so despite the chill, those two decided to walk to the shops to get some fish and chips for our supper.

Around five o'clock, Jason said he was going to walk to town. He wanted to play in his usual darts competition at the pub. Feeling a bit concerned, I asked him to wait for Tedo to come and get him and take him down there in the car. Impatient to get on his way, Jason said he would start walking. I called to Aimon to go to his Uncle Tedo's and ask him to pick Jason up on the main road to town. Aimon took off running.

For a reason I couldn't explain, I went out to the front porch where I stood and watched Jason walk out of our yard and down to the corner. He must have felt me still watching him because at that moment he turned, saw me and waved. I waved back before he went out of sight behind our neighbour's fence.

I went back inside and curled up on our couch. Then, strangely out of character, our tough little Alison came and cuddled up with me. Usually she would be off playing with her friends who lived next door. It was a bit unusual, but I didn't question it. I just cuddled my daughter closer.

About ten minutes later, Aimon burst through the front door, shouting at the top of his little voice, 'Mum! Mum! Uncle Tedo's taken Dad to the hospital!' Putting Alison to one side, I quickly got up from the couch. I could see he was in shock, so I grabbed him and asked him to tell me what happened. Through short breaths and tears flooding his eyes he cried, 'Mum, we found Dad on the ground at the garage when we went to pick him up. Now they at the hospital.'

Feeling very scared, I turned to Jason Junior and shouted at him to look after his brothers and sister.

I sprinted barefoot out the yard, across the main road, down the gravel pathway and into the hospital grounds. I ran straight into the main entrance and down the corridor towards Emergency.

Out of nowhere, I was stopped in my tracks by Tedo. I could see he was crying, but he gripped me by both shoulders and stopped me going any further. I struggled to break his grip, my arms flailing everywhere, screaming loudly.

I continued to struggle to get free until Tedo tearfully pleaded with me, 'No, sis, please don't go there. Please. It's not something you want to see. He's at peace now.'

I backed away from Tedo, shaking my head in utter disbelief, sinking to the cold floor of the hospital. My mind was racing as I cried out for him. Jason. The man whose life had always been linked with mine. The man whose name I carried. We had been to hell and back in our time together. We finally had a real future, going forward with our children. He can't be gone.

I don't know how long I lay there. As if in a dream, a nurse came and gave me a drink of water. Then she and a still tearful Tedo helped me to my feet. I turned when I heard someone else screaming. Leira, Old Ted, Patty and Gwenda came towards me. We held on to each other, crying and praying it wasn't true.

The doctor who delivered our first two sons came out to see us a few seconds later. We all turned to him, muffling our sobs, holding our breath. He just shook his head. His expression was very grave. He came over, put his hand on my shoulder and said, 'I am so very sorry, Lavinia. He had a massive heart attack. We did everything possible, but we couldn't save him.'

I leaned heavily on Leira. Her strength barely supported us both. Like the sound of a final siren signalling utter defeat, our wailing echoed through the long hospital corridors.

HAVE TO GO

How people change. When Jason was still alive, even though we had been apart for several years before getting back together for the last two years of his life, there was always a kind of unvoiced acknowledgement that our four kids and I belonged to him. It was as if there was an unwritten Nyoongar code that no one would hassle us or they would have to deal with him. In our Nyoongar community, it was a prospect few would dare to test out. So no one ever said anything bad about us, at least not to our faces. But following Jason's passing, it wasn't long before the knives came out.

At twenty-nine years old, I was no longer an inexperienced girl. In those nearly three decades of being part of this universe, I had already survived enough trauma to last a lifetime. I had been through some very tough times and I had emerged a bit damaged, but much stronger. But nobody else seemed to recognise this. It seemed everyone wanted to give me advice on what to do, including Jason's white mates and their wives, to whom I had hardly ever spoken.

First, they offered their commiserations. The next time we met, they offered suggestions. This usually happened when I bumped into them while out shopping. Oh, they were very kind and always asked if we were okay, did we have enough money, did we need food or anything? But then came the advice on what I should do. And sometimes even what I shouldn't be doing. It wasn't as if I hadn't been getting the same thing from my own family and in-laws now that Jason was gone.

Then there was the Nyoongar community and their advice. A charitable way of looking at it would be to think that the Nyoongar community was missing Jason too, but mostly it felt like they were going to give advice whether I asked for it or not. Even worse was when Jason's male so-called 'friends', white and black, offered to help me tend to more than our lawn. A lot of them were married and after the initial shock of each offer, I told those arseholes to fuck off.

Jason's funeral had been tough, but we all went through it mostly numb. In the first few months afterwards, I threw myself into looking after my four kids. Getting them off to school every day during the week and taking them to play footy or basketball on the weekends. There were always a few of their young cousins with us as well. They would often sleep over after their games and head home the next day. Also, for a long while we still attended church to catch up with our 'out of town' relatives. It seemed to me every day, and sometimes overnight, our home was never short of kids. In a way it was good because I never had time to think about things too much and I kept myself busy with my children, my house and my own sports.

My nephew Tony and his wife, Lola, were still staying with us and I appreciated the adult company. I also found time to spend with my Uncle Levi. He was a widower, having lost Aunty May some years ago. He was still very active and would walk to town and back every day. I used to keep telling him to let me know if he wanted to get picked up and I would drive him into town. In some ways he became my 'go-to person' if I needed to talk to someone. I knew whatever I said to him would go no further. That was a rare thing in our small Nyoongar community where everybody knew everyone else's business.

There were other changes going on too, with my dad moving to Spearwood to stay with my sister Hannah and her husband. Also, Lucy had signed on at Curtin University to further her community health nursing career. As a result, she and her husband were given accommodation on campus. Before they left, they gave their dog, Sparky, to Aimon to look after because there was no room for dwerts in their small student apartment. Sparky followed Aimon everywhere he went and we had to tie him up so Aimon could leave for school every morning.

When I had time to myself, my mind was in turmoil. I found it hard to believe that Jason had really gone. I went from feeling sorry for myself and my children, to being angry and questioning God. I came to believe that God presents us with some challenges that will make or break us. It's like those trials and tribulations were put there to give us a taste of what the future might hold. It seemed as if those early hardships are just a training run. So if and when we get through those, then we are given even more of life's hurdles. We have two choices – either get over them or stumble.

The final realisation that Jason was never coming back came quite unexpectedly. Late one night I was sitting alone watching television in the lounge room after everyone else was in bed. I must have dozed off because I woke suddenly and realised that Jason's favourite show, *Alvin Purple*, had started. Still half asleep and without thinking, I jumped up and walked toward our bedroom calling out, 'Jason, your show is on. You gunna watch it?'

The door was slightly ajar and when I swung it open and switched on the light, all that was there was our empty bed. I started sobbing. I cried for Jason, the young bloke who I had known since childhood. The man who chose to marry me. Chose me to be the mother of his children. The man who betrayed me. Who came back and worked hard to rebuild a good relationship together. I lay on the floor by the empty bed and accepted that Jason was gone.

It finally became too much. As a single woman again, I grew tired of the constant interrogation by those who had no right to question me. No right to dictate to me. I decided to leave Pinjarra. To some people it would never be right. For instance, even what I wore was being commented upon. I was wearing trackies at home and to training, and a uniform that everyone else on the team was wearing whenever I played sport. Yet I was accused of, and targeted by my sister-in-law Patty, as flashing my body around. A person can't win.

It finally came to a head one day after I had dropped off the two oldest kids at school. I had pulled up near the park and was walking towards the shops. Pat came rushing up to me, swearing loudly and showing her fists. When she got close, she swung a punch at me.

I ducked and pushed her back. She was much bigger than me but slower, so it was easy to avoid the next lot of punches she threw my way. I kept asking her what was her problem but she was relentless. In an effort to get away from Pat, I found myself in front of a light pole just as she chucked a roundhouse punch at my face. I ducked and she hit the pole full-on. She screamed out in pain as her hand connected to the wood with some force. She doubled over, clutching her wrist and hand, saying I had broken her arm.

I didn't care. I just walked back to the car and drove off. I made up my mind that I was leaving Pinjarra for good. I wasn't sure where I would go.

I told my Uncle Levi first, then let my nephew Tony know what I was going to do and told him that he and Lola could stay there until I applied for a transfer. They were already on State Housing lists seeking accommodation for themselves, so maybe the government would let them stay longer. I said he could have my furniture because there was no way I could take it with me. The only things I packed in my car were our clothes, some toys, important papers and family photographs.

As soon as school finished that day, I picked up my children and we headed for Spearwood. I didn't know where else to go. Both Jono and Hannah were living there, so maybe I could stay with one of them for a while. Their houses were only a few kilometres apart, but both were near shops and schools.

I pulled in at Hannah's first because Dad was living with her and her family and I wanted to let him know what had happened. Not long after we arrived her husband, Nicky, came home from work and, as usual, he and Hannah got into a right royal slanging match. That was enough for me to pack the kids back into the car and head for Jono's place.

By the time we got there, it was nearly sundown. My kids were happy to catch up with Jono's kids. Dot was not there. She had gone to a funeral, but was due back later that night. It gave me a chance to talk with Jono about us staying with him for a while. Just until I got my own house. After I explained what was happening in Pinjarra, Jono agreed that we could stay with his family until my transfer came through.

I heard on the Nyoongar grapevine that a lot of people thought it strange that I had taken myself and my children to live with my brother and his wife when there had previously been so much bad blood between us.

But as Jono said, 'As far as I'm concerned that's in the past now. Dot has changed, she's not drinking anymore. We're okay. So, sis, you and my niece and nephews are welcome to stay until you get your own place.'

Strange as it might sound, there were never any complaints from Dot. I think she enjoyed us all being there. After all, my four koolungahs belonged to Jason. And sometimes, I really thought she still loved him. My kids were a part of him and she made them welcome.

It took about two months before I was given a transfer from the house in Pinjarra. It came through fairly quickly because I reminded State Housing of Shane's health issues. With the support of the social worker assigned to us from the hospital and a letter of support from a senior officer at the state Aboriginal Affairs Planning Authority – a new name for Native Welfare – we were given a priority listing.

Those agencies agreed that we should not be living in an overcrowded house, so we were allocated one in Willagee. My dad moved in with us as well because he believed I needed support with my boys since Jason Junior was now thirteen years old, and Aimon was nearly twelve. In addition, my niece Nita moved in too. She was nearly eighteen and starting to spread her adult wings. By staying with us, she was female company for me and my daughter, had the safety of her own family, and her extra income helped us with food and board.

As a family, although my kids and I were starting from scratch in terms of setting up a home, it felt fantastic. That old four-bedroom state house was another symbol of moving on with my life. Of my independence. No more living in other people's homes. No more sleeping on some relative's floor. I had my own room and my own bed. My niece and daughter shared one room, the boys had their own room and Dad had his. Most of all, I had peace of mind.

The day we moved in I felt things were definitely looking up. I was still involved with my sport. I played netball on the weekends and basketball two nights a week in different local competitions. Other evenings I trained. I was so physically fit I amazed even myself. Every day I thanked God for my good health. I was also grateful that I had my own vehicle. It enabled me to take all four kids with me, though there were a few times the two older ones opted to stay home with Dad.

In late 1979 I was asked again to try out for the Aboriginal State Netball team. I attended the elimination games in Midland and was chosen in the final cut of ten players. I was gobsmacked when I was picked by the selectors to captain the side. That year Western Australia celebrated one hundred and fifty years of white settlement. So it was seen as fitting to host the national Aboriginal netball and football carnivals in Perth.

Each day of the carnival a lot of my family members came to watch me play. They barracked wicked for me and our team. They definitely were the loudest bunch on the sidelines. I was so proud because my dad turned up for every game I played in. He watched on when I was presented with the Captain's Medallion from that year. Also a small runner-up trophy for our team's loss in the Grand Final, again against New South Wales.

As well as playing sport and caring for my family, I enrolled in a secretarial course. It was not so intense or as time consuming as the teaching degree and I managed to finish that off in only six months. The course was held right in the city, so to save money on fuel and parking, I travelled by bus. It was a full-time course but some days I only had to attend for two hours. Being so flexible, that particular course worked for me. It meant I would always be home when my kids got back from school each afternoon.

I received top marks in my final assessment, with high passes in business English, bookkeeping, shorthand and typing. I didn't go straight into work though because I wanted to spend time with my children. And with my widow's pension and family support benefit, my niece's board money and Dad's pension, I didn't need to find a job straight away. I even managed to pay off my car.

One weekend when we all had time off from our sports, I took them to Boddington to a country rodeo and fair. As well as all the stalls and electronic bull riding, on offer was a ride in a crop duster plane. I had enough money to take the five of us on the flight. The pilot flew all around the hills and valleys and along the course of the Hotham River. Though it was only a small plane – and the ride only lasted about thirty minutes – it was amazing. None of the kids had ever been in a plane before. Looking down, we felt as if we were on top of the world.

PORTER

It was about twelve months after I became a widow that I started going out on different occasions with my sister, my niece, some cousins or a few close friends. It was mostly to family gatherings – weddings and birthdays, or community events. And I often took my children with me to basketball carnivals. I still played both netball and basketball and I made a lot of new friends. I did meet a few single men in all that socialising. There was one I really liked, but when I heard through the good old Nyoongar grapevine that he had gotten another woman pregnant, I steered right away from him. Besides, a few were a bit young for me. I already had four children and had no intention of being a 'mummy figure' to anyone else. Unfortunately, all the ones around my age were married up so they were part of a definite 'no-go zone'. I even mentioned to my dad that it seemed like I might be single for the rest of my life.

Then I met Porter. I remember that day very well. I was visiting a good friend, Jill, to catch up with all the latest Nyoongar gossip. We didn't have mobile phones back then, let alone social media like Facebook. Shortly after I got to her house, she asked if I wanted to come for a ride to visit her aunty. I had nothing else planned for the day – my kids had gone on holidays to Pinjarra with their uncle Tedo – so I went with her to Armadale.

When we pulled up to her auntie's house and walked inside,

a bloke called out from the kitchen asking if we wanted tea or coffee.

'Tea!' we called back.

I entered the lounge room and the first thing I noticed was how high all the family photos were on the walls. I had to look up just to see them. The house was very neat and tidy, like a display home. Ornaments, trophies and photos filled all the shelves. The voice from the other room called out again, inviting us to grab a seat at the kitchen table, so I followed Jill through.

The bloke had his back to us, facing the sink, but I could see he was really tall. No wonder the photos were hung up high. He turned around, holding two cups of tea that he placed on the table in front of us.

'Grab a seat and help yourself to milk and sugar. I'll just get some biscuits.'

Jill said, 'Here, cuz, this is my friend Lavinia. Lavinia, this is my cousin Porter.'

We shook hands and I couldn't help but notice that his huge hand completely covered my own. He was really good-looking – tall, dark and handsome.

Jill asked where her aunt – Porter's mum – was, only to be told she had gone shopping with her sister. He said he wasn't sure when she would be back. Another bloke appeared from the backyard. Jill told me he was their cousin Gordon. He was blind but you wouldn't know it. He certainly knew his way around the house.

The afternoon passed with Porter, Jill and Gordon catching up with their family news. There was a lot of laughter between them. Time flew by. Then Porter cooked a stew and made a dampa to go with it, so we decided to stay for a feed. His mum hadn't returned by then, so Jill and I left to go back to her place.

That was it. Nothing spectacular. I did find it easy to talk with Porter, and even tease him, but there were no sparks going off that day. He came across as a very funny, friendly, awfully good-looking younger bloke who knew how to cook a lovely meal and then clean up. Also, I assumed he had a wife or at least a girlfriend somewhere in the background.

As a single mother who moved in different circles, I didn't expect to ever see him again. I did put a few questions to Jill about him, but she wasn't giving out too much at all. I did find out he was single.

It must have been a month later that I received an invitation to my niece Nita's eighteenth birthday party from her parents. The school holidays would be on and I knew my kids had already lined it up to go to their Uncle Tedo's place in Pinjarra. And Dad had made other plans. It seemed I would be at a loose end, so I let Nita and her parents know I would be coming to celebrate with her.

A few days later I asked Jill if she wanted to join me at the birthday party. She and her man had other plans, but her teenage girls had also received an invite to Nita's party and Jill asked if I could drop them off afterwards. I was surprised when she also gave me Porter's phone number and suggested I ask him to go if I wanted company.

I was a bit apprehensive, because I hardly knew him at all, but I remembered how easygoing he was when we first met. So over the next couple of weeks I asked a few more people, including my brother-in-law, what they knew about him. Tedo said he knew Porter's brothers Mal and Pete. He told me that his cousin Vida was married to Mal, and that he and my cousin Rick had played footy with Pete in the Western Australian Aboriginal state teams. Further research on my part revealed that everybody I spoke to thought Porter was a decent person. I found out he was a plumber and a hard worker. That he was a really good footy player, liked a cold beer and was a respectable sort of bloke. He'd been living in Victoria and had returned to the west not long ago. He was about twenty-six and definitely single. No wife. No girlfriend of any consequence.

I took Porter's phone number from Jill and bit the bullet. I rang him a few days before the party. He accepted, saying that someone would drop him off, so we agreed for him to meet me there. All my mob who turned up were curious about him. Some too curious. Four of my female cousins said if I didn't want him to please, please send him their way. We had a really good time, dancing and partying on, and towards the end I drove Jill's girls home. When I got back to the party, I couldn't see Porter anywhere. When we first arrived, him being six feet six inches tall, he stood out amidst my shorter relatives. But now he was nowhere to be seen.

Oh well, I thought. Win some, lose some. He must have gone off with one of my cousins. Without another thought about him, I headed straight for the kitchen to help with the cleaning up. My sister Lucy asked what I was doing. She told me, 'Lavinia, go back to your friend.'

I told her I couldn't see him anywhere, he must have gone. She gave me a funny look, but I just shrugged and started doing the wiping up. About ten minutes later, I went into the main hall to collect some more dirty dishes. Behind a table in the corner, there he was, sitting on the floor with one of my nephews, yarning their heads off. Talking music and no doubt telling each other all sorts of bullshit.

He hadn't left. When he saw me, he jumped up and gave me an unexpected hug. He kissed me on the forehead. He must have thought I had left him in the lurch with all my mad mob.

We both started laughing. Our laughter was definitely tinged with a bit of relief on both our parts. He had his ride home, and I was glad he had waited for me. On the way out, I saw Lucy smiling at me before giving me both thumbs up.

On the way to his house, I asked if he wanted to stop at my niece's house in Kelmscott for a little while. At the birthday party, she had asked me if I wanted to go to her 'after party' for a feed and a few drinks. 'No worries,' he said. When we arrived, there were only three other cars parked in her yard. We went inside and spent the next hour or so eating pizza and drinking cool drinks. We ended up staying at her place for the night. We slept on her crowded lounge room floor. I really can't explain it. At the age of thirty-one, being there and spending time with Porter felt like I had actually found home.

Porter and I kept on seeing each other. He was still living at home in Armadale with his mum. That worked out well for both of them – he was good company for her and he was working for a plumbing company in Roleystone, which was less than ten minutes' drive from his house.

Sometimes he came over and stayed for the weekend with us, but it was about six months before he finally moved in and stayed. He got on really well with Dad and my kids, though he did clash once with Jason Junior. We sorted that out with some pretty strict ground rules for all of us.

Apart from being tall, dark and handsome, Porter was a gentleman. He was also well educated and would tell wicked jokes that made everyone laugh. It always put people at ease, though I would pull him up if they got too smutty and rude. He worked hard and liked a beer. Like me, he was definitely into music. Unlike me his choice was loud headbanging music. Poxy Led Zeppelin music.

What I did like was his wanting to be around me. I knew he had strong feelings for me and he always bought me gifts. I had rarely had that happen before. Someone buying me gifts out of the blue. He just wanted to get me something nice.

It wasn't love at first sight, maybe a bit of lust, but just being with him made me feel good. There was no emotional stress at all. It felt like it was meant to be.

NOT TO BE

Being teenagers by now, my sons were fast turning into young men. Shane had also grown taller. Even though he had put on a few inches in height, his older brothers didn't like him hanging around them. They had discovered girls, so at times Shane was left out. My daughter also had her school friends over so it made for some crowded but happy times. It was good for me to have Porter and Dad there to make sure things didn't get out of hand. Especially with some of those hot-tempered, testosterone-filled young fullas.

We had been together for nearly two years when Porter and I decided to try to have a baby. After Shane was born I had had my tubes tied, so in order to get pregnant again I would need to have that medically reversed. Porter and I had to undergo all sorts of tests. We had a lot of laughter about what he had to do to get the specimens for testing. Finally, after that corrective surgery, four months later, I became pregnant. We were so happy when we told our families. Making plans and deciding on names was an exciting time.

One morning, it must have been about two o'clock, I was woken by someone touching my shoulder. I turned over and faced the other way. This time someone shook my shoulder. In the dim light, I looked around our room to see who it was. Nobody was there. Porter was with me in bed and he was snoring. I couldn't explain it, even to myself. I lay awake for about twenty minutes, in which time I could feel a strong invisible presence right next to me. It wasn't going away and I sensed something was seriously wrong. I just couldn't put my finger on what it might be.

Following my instincts, I shook Porter and woke him up. I told him I wanted to go to King Edward Hospital right now. He wanted to know why but I couldn't tell him because I didn't know myself. I told him, 'Let's just go now please, mate.' We woke Dad and told him what had happened. He told us to go. He would look after things at home.

We got to the hospital about half an hour later. Being nearly thirteen weeks pregnant, the nurses in the emergency department started doing all sorts of tests and asking the usual round of questions. Are you in pain? No. Are you bleeding? No. Have you been injured? No. And I didn't have a temperature.

The unspoken question was, Lavinia, why are you here then? The medical staff decided to book me in for more comprehensive tests. Porter stayed with me and, about seven o'clock that morning, rang his boss to tell him what had happened and he wouldn't be in until later.

Two hours later, after undergoing numerous blood and urine tests, x-rays and even an ultrasound, I was finally visited by a specialist. He looked at my chart and then the x-rays. He turned to the nurses accompanying him and almost shouted at one to get the operating theatre ready. Now!

He asked when I had last eaten, then told the other nurse to prepare me for immediate surgery. Porter and I looked at each other. It sounded really serious. The doctor only said he needed to operate on me at once. Nothing else. Bewildered and somewhat scared, we didn't even get a chance to ask any more questions. The doctor walked out. We could hear him telling the nurse to call the surgery support staff and to cancel the rest of his round for the morning. I don't know if anyone had spoken to Porter about what was going to happen. I do remember signing papers for the procedure to go ahead just before I was wheeled into surgery.

I woke up late in the afternoon. Through groggy eyes, I could see Porter sitting on the chair near my bed. He leaned over and kissed me on the cheek. Still holding my hand, he asked if I wanted a drink. Apart from that, we didn't speak at all. There was no need for words. I took a sip, then the tears came. Porter took the glass and set it on the table, then reached over and hugged me.

Soon after, the specialist came to see us. He told us that we had lost our baby. He wanted to know what made me come in that morning. I had shown none of the usual signs of trouble with the pregnancy. Without waiting for a reply, he told me it was very lucky that I had come in when I had. If I had left an hour longer, I would have died. I had had an ectopic pregnancy. The baby was growing in my fallopian tubes and scarring on the tubes from previous pregnancies meant this baby couldn't make his way through to my womb.

He explained that if our baby had kept growing, he would have eventually burst my fallopian tube and I would have had life-threatening internal bleeding. In a very serious tone, the doctor told us that I had actually come within an hour of dying.

I was kept in hospital for a couple of days. I felt devastated. Losing our baby like that left me deeply saddened. Physically I got better, but emotionally I was shattered. I mourned in silence for months. Porter was there for me, as were my dad and children. But they couldn't really understand the psychological and emotional turmoil that I was going through. He was part of my body and I grieved alone.

I still don't know who touched me on the shoulder that night. Who had woken me up and told me to get to the hospital. In our Nyoongar culture, my mum always told us that old spirits look after each and every one of us. I put it down to my guardian spirits.

ALL GROWN UP

Time marched on and it wasn't long before Jason Junior and Aimon were now in their mid-teens and becoming really independent. Alison was in high school and Shane was doing well in primary school. On the odd weekend, Dad would be off visiting one of his other children for a couple of days. Our lives revolved around school, sport and making sure Dad kept his doctor appointments.

Sport was still high on our family agenda. My three sons were playing for the local footy club and doing very well. Every season they brought home trophies. Alison was into netball and played at the East Fremantle courts along with Ginny, her younger cousin. Our family expanded a bit when my nephews Rodney and Gary – who as a baby had lived with us in Pinjarra – came to stay with us again in Willagee. It was lovely to have him around, being part of our family again. Having the two nephews living with us never bothered Dad and in fact he often got the older ones to run errands for him.

There was one young wadjerlar boy in particular who always seemed to be around. Gazza became friends with Aimon when he was about ten or eleven years old. He spent more time at our place than his own home. He would often come around and we would see that he was very upset. We didn't pry, but made sure he had a feed. I advised Aimon to keep an eye on him after he told us he was sick of living. Then one day, after some major altercation with his family, he moved into our place and he has been a part of our family ever since.

With all the young ones coming around following my pied-piper children, Porter and I laid down more ground rules and there was never any trouble. I remember one weekend when there were about fourteen kids at our place. Nyoongar kids and wadjerlar kids. Girls and boys. They often hung around until late on Sundays. We managed to feed them all, and after they had eaten, they all pitched in to clean up.

Alison had grown into a beautiful young lady and she always had a lot of her girlfriends over. Of course the boys would try and impress them whenever they gathered at our place.

But Alison was a no-nonsense person and she could barely stand the friends of her older brothers. They never said anything stupid or step out of line with her. If they did, she would have punched into them herself, or her brothers and cousins would have dealt with them. Whichever way, her brother's friends respected her.

But there was one young chap that she did like. Patrick was a Nyoongar boy about Alison's age and he used to travel from his home in Gosnells over to Willagee and stay with relatives who lived not far from our house. He even signed up to play in the local footy team with our sons. When we met him, we could see that he was keen on our daughter. He came back practically every weekend and eventually asked for our permission to take Alison out. After laying down a few strict rules, we gave them the okay.

Unlike Patrick, who had a home and big family who cared about him, I do believe some of the young people who came to our place were street kids. For whatever reason, they couldn't get on with their families. They turned up every weekend. Our sons explained that a few of them had been physically abused by their parents or foster parents.

One Sunday, a young boy aged about seven came to see Shane and they spent the afternoon playing board games at our place.

This young chap was a few years younger than Shane and went to the same primary school. He lived in Willagee, so just before dark Shane and Alison walked him back to his place. The next afternoon, after school, he turned up at our house again looking for Shane. When I saw him, I was horrified. The poor little bugger had bruises on his face, legs and arms. I asked Shane about it and he informed me that the little fulla's stepdad had flogged him. It wasn't the first time this had happened.

While the boy stayed with Shane at our place, I had Porter take me to their house. After I knocked a few times, this ugly, skinny bloke came to the door. After I introduced myself, but before he even had a chance to answer, I called him a dirty, cowardly bully. I told him if I ever saw bruises on the little seven-year-old boy again two things would happen. The first was I would report him to the authorities. The second was I would come down with a baseball bat and flog the fuck out of him. I was so angry. I told him if there were any more bruising on the boy I would be back. And I wouldn't be coming alone.

There were never any more reports from Shane about bruising on the little bloke, thank God. He still came up over every now and then. But I later heard his mother had taken him interstate to get away from the stepdad.

Soon after that, when he was seventeen, Jason Junior left school and started work at a garage in Mount Pleasant. We were pretty proud of him because after he was there for a while, he was given the run of the place. He liked messing around working on cars, so it suited him to a tee. And he was getting paid to do it. There was even talk of him becoming an apprentice mechanic, but six months later the garage changed hands and the new owners didn't keep him on. Both he and Aimon were still involved in playing footy and we had scouts from South Fremantle come out and watch them play with a view to signing them on.

Then Aimon started getting into trouble with the police. Mainly for minor misdemeanours, but it wasn't a good thing to have the police coming around asking where he was all the time. Then at fifteen, he left school. He told us he no longer had any interest in studying and he didn't want to be in the classroom, so he started work with my cousin Rick promoting our Nyoongar culture through dance and theatre. He took to the work like a duck to water. He turned up for rehearsals and performances on time every day. Later, he was joined by Jason Junior and together they travelled all around the state performing. Rick looked after them and they were kept busy working with his company.

Around that time, Porter was invited to join his brothers to play country football in Hyden, about 330 kilometres south-east of Perth. He would be paid to play, which was good because it was about a three-hour drive there and back, and fuel was getting pretty expensive.

So every Sunday we'd head to Hyden or wherever their match was being played. Sometimes we took Alison and Shane with us, leaving the two older sons to be company for Dad.

The only downside of Porter playing football with his brothers was they always had a booze up afterwards. Sometimes when that happened, I noticed he would get a bit nasty towards me. Jealous even. I couldn't understand why it was happening because usually after a few beers he would just relax. Up until then, we got on so well. This behaviour seemed so out of character for him. Over the next couple of months, it got worse. I couldn't even go to the shop without him quizzing me about why I had taken so long.

I hated his distrust of me and I was becoming increasingly annoyed with it. I'd had enough of that crap in my life before I met him. I certainly didn't need it now. Then one day he came home drunk. He started with the accusations, jealousy and even calling me some pretty abusive names. I told him to pack his bags and piss off out of my life. Then Dad, my kids and I took off for Jono's place. He followed us, and when he pulled up outside Jono's house, he started yelling and cursing me all over again.

I had had enough! I grabbed my nephew's baseball bat and went out to confront him, quite prepared to bash him with it. Jono stopped me, then turned to Porter and told him to go along or the police would be called. He took off, and I didn't hear a word for about three weeks. I did hear he was back with his mum and she had blasted him for how he had carried on.

Then one day, he turned up. Stone-cold sober. He apologised to me and said he wanted to come back. I told him there was no way I would take him back as long as he was still drinking alcohol. It was either me or the long brown bottle. He said he didn't want us to break up. I didn't want that either, but there was no way I was going to put up with any drunken crap from him. I knew I could and would survive without him. He knew it too. I told him I would give him two months to get clean, to prove he was serious about giving up the booze. Then I would consider it. We left it at that.

Two weeks later, Porter came over and had a barbecue with me, Dad and my family and Jono's. He was sober and he looked good. He asked to stay, but I said no. It must have been about six weeks later when he announced he had been sober all that time and asked if it was now okay to come back to Willagee and be with us. After some really serious discussion, I agreed and he came back home on one condition. No alcohol! He has never touched any since then.

Don't get me wrong. Over the years, we've had some arguments, disagreements and heated debates. I have even sworn at him in several languages, but there has never been any violence or threats of violence, and we sorted things out so much easier because he was sober. As a reward to himself for giving up the booze, he got a loan and bought a brand-new, bright red Holden ute. It was a magnificent piece of machinery. Flashy in appearance and with a V8 engine. It was certainly noticed when out on the road.

It wasn't too long after that when one day in her second year at high school, Ali came home with a detention notice and a request for me to meet with her form teacher because she had been involved in a fight. I followed through and went up to the school. I was shown into an office and, along with my daughter, waited for her teacher, Mr Simmons. When he walked through the door, I could see he was a big man about the same height as Porter.

After a curt hello, he started to tell me why he had given Alison detention. He said she had gotten into a fight with three boys. The school didn't allow that sort of behaviour. All this time he was practically standing over us, barking out the information, trying to intimidate us.

I turned to Alison and asked why she had punched into those three boys. She said, 'Mum, as I told Mr Simmons, one called me a black bitch, one called me a black slut and the other burst out laughing at their insults. That's why I punched into them.'

I asked Alison if they had hit her. She said they had tried, but they were too slow. She had given two of the boys black eyes and the other one a cut lip and a nose bleed. Then they had run and reported her to the teacher.

I don't think he expected me to react the way I did. I stood straight up and squared off with him. My teacher training was put to good use that day. I had been trained how to deal with irate parents, how to get the upper hand. I wasn't going to let him use some psychological bullshit to intimidate me. I stared him right in the face and I didn't take one step backwards. I said straight out, 'So

Mr Simmons, you knew they had sworn at my daughter. You knew they tried to hit her. And have they been punished for that? Have they been suspended from school?'

He glared, but his silence spoke volumes. I went on, 'So they get off scot-free for threatening and swearing at my daughter and you do nothing? I tell you what. Tomorrow I'll get my husband, Porter, to come down and discuss this with you. Talk man to man, instead of you talking down and trying to intimidate me and my girl.'

Still staring right at him, I spoke to Alison, 'Mr Simmons, you should hear this. Alison, that's good you stuck up for yourself. Don't ever let anyone insult you. Good job you punched into those three stupid idiots. And calling you black?'

I turned to face him again and said, 'You do know there are new laws against discrimination and we will look further into that, Mr Simmons. My husband and I will be back first thing in the morning and you can discuss that with him too.'

Before he could say anything further, I said, 'Let's go Alison. You got another two days off. Let Porter sort this out with Mr Simmons tomorrow.'

The next day, both Porter and I went to the same office and when Mr Simmons walked in and saw that Porter was more than a match for him, his whole manner changed from yesterday. He practically grovelled. No raised voice, no standover intimidation tactics, only apologising and promising those three boys would be punished.

All Porter said was, 'I hope so, Mr Simmons. I would hate to have to come back here for something like this. Our daughter deserves to be treated better than that.'

The only comment we got from him was a very meek, 'Thank you for coming in, Mr Hasluck.'

SHIFTING PLACES

The decision to move to Armadale came about because Porter worked in Roleystone and it was costing us a lot for him to travel nearly forty kilometres there and back to Willagee every day. He had to drive to his boss's house, pick up the company vehicle and go to his first call-out location.

It wasn't difficult to transfer Alison and Shane across to their new school which was within close walking distance of the place State Housing allocated us. Dad came too but, being old and set in his ways, he didn't change his bank or his doctor until months later. It meant every fortnight we'd travel to Fremantle so he could do his banking and see his doctor for a check-up. We did this because we appreciated that he was getting old and needed to make those changes when it suited him.

The day we moved into the new place in Armadale, we were amazed at the rubbish that was still lying around the yard. It looked like the previous tenants were a rough lot. State Housing had done a token effort at cleaning, but that was simply filling in a few deep holes and raking over where a fire had been lit to burn rubbish. When setting up our garden beds in both the front and back yards, Porter and the young fullas had to dig down about one meter before they reached good soil. Before they reached that level, they found the ground was packed with bottle tops, broken glass, plastic, cardboard, ashes and other unknown dirty material. The blokes borrowed a back hoe and dug out the crap, then levelled everything with new clean soil. Once they planted some decent lawn that too was covered with yellow sand to help the grass come through.

We were only there for a week when two car loads of Nyoongar men pull up in front of our yard. At the time, only Dad and I were there. I watched through the window as one young bloke got out of the car and came to the door. When he knocked, I answered it. Standing there was one of my nephews. He seemed shocked to see me there.

'Aunty Lavinia, what are you doing here?'

'We moved in here last week. Why Jock, who you looking for?'

'No one, Aunt. We just cruising. You don't know where those fullas who used to live here have moved to?'

'No, sorry, bub.'

With that he turned and signalled to the blokes in the car that whoever they were looking for was no longer living here. As he got into the car he looked back and waved.

I found out later that those blokes had come to fight the previous tenants. Apparently, an ongoing feud existed between two local Nyoongar families. It had been going on for some time and the two car loads we saw had come to clash with them as payback. I thanked God it was my nephew who came to the door and not somebody who didn't know me. They might have started on me and Dad by mistake.

Our household settled into some sort of routine with Porter going to work, Alison, Shane and Gary off to school and Jason Junior, Aimon and Rodney heading into the city to work with their Uncle Rick and his group. Gazza, the boy's wadjerlar mate from Willagee, turned up a few times each week and he joined the young blokes as well. Dad was home with me and I was glad of his company.

It was mid-week and I had just dished up supper for everyone. Nine plates. Porter was due home from work any minute. We heard the ute pull up, so I added a tenth plate to the table. Porter came in the front door, holding a bunch of pretty flowers. He came over, gave me a kiss and then the flowers. There was a chorus of 'yuck' from the young ones, then laughter. Porter told them, 'Get used to it, you lot.' Turning to me he added, 'Lavinia, will you marry me?'

I sat down and began eating my meal. I was only half listening to what Porter was saying, so I said, 'Yeah, I'll marry you, now sit down and eat your supper.'

Still standing near me, this time Porter spoke a bit louder. 'Lavinia, will *you marry me?*'

Suddenly, there was silence right around the table. They had picked up on the importance of the question and didn't want to miss my response.

I looked at him. Incredulously, I asked, 'You mean it, don't you?'

'Yes I do, mate.'

Dad said, 'Lavinia, answer the man.'

I paused for about two seconds before I stood up and said out loud, 'Yes! Yes I will!'

Porter hugged me, then gave me another big kiss. More shouts of 'yuck' from the young ones.

Dad raised his mug of tea and said, 'Cheers, you two.'

He was joined by everyone sitting around the table.

It wasn't like one of those proposals in the movies, but I did get the flowers and more importantly, approval by all those who mattered so much to me. Porter later went to see his mum to tell her the good news.

Over the next few months, things got quite hectic. Getting married sounded so simple but unlike my first wedding, where everything was taken care of by my family, this time there was so much more planning for us to do. For our part, Porter and I had to find a church and a preacher, then provide all sorts of legal papers to him. We originally wanted to get married at the Anglican church in Maddington because it was really close to the local community hall where we were planning the reception. But that church was being renovated, so it was decided to use a church in Gosnells.

That day in April seemed to roll around very quickly. It was quite different to my first wedding, and luckily I had plenty of help from Alison, Lucy and Hannah. They were the three I asked to be my maid of honour and bridesmaids. Lucy especially made time to drive us around, choosing the wedding gown, bridesmaid dresses, the cake and flowers. There were only a few formal invitations sent out. Like most Nyoongar weddings in those days, if relatives made the effort to turn up and witness the nuptials, they would be welcome. Somewhere in all of the planning, Hannah asked if her daughter Ginny could be in the wedding party instead of herself. I had no complaints about the change and Porter's young niece, Tiffany, agreed to be my flower girl.

The wedding gown I chose was beautiful. It was full length, made of white Chantilly lace with an off-the-shoulder neckline. I had wrist-length white lace gloves and a small hat with a mid-length veil cascading down my back. I had my hair, make-up and nails done by my nieces. When I saw my reflection in the mirror, I hardly recognised myself. I had never looked so beautiful. I started to get a bit emotional but Lucy grounded me.

'No tears, Lavinia. You'll ruin your make-up.' Despite her words, both she and Hannah looked like they were going to shed a tear too. Fortunately, Alison, Ginny and Tiffany came bustling into the room telling us it was time to go and get some photos.

Lucy's son Tim, who happened to be a police officer, was the designated photographer, and when we came out of the house, he greeted us with a big wolf whistle. He immediately began organising us so he could take the best shots. We were then joined by Dad, Jason Junior and Aimon. They had scrubbed up really well in their hired suits. For a few minutes, we took various poses while Tim clicked away. Then the transport arrived and our group was whisked away to the church.

I was surprised by the number of people who had come to our wedding. A lot of them were standing outside the church. I thought they were waiting to go in. But when I entered the church, it was already packed. Standing room only! I looked to where Porter was up the front with the preacher and he smiled when he saw me come in. He had been joined by his two brothers and Shane. I barely noticed them because I had eyes for only one man.

Jason Junior walked me down the aisle and stood beside me until everyone had settled down and the preacher indicated for him to take a step back. When we were pronounced husband and wife and introduced to the congregation as Mr and Mrs Hasluck, Porter then gave me the biggest kiss. The whole church erupted to cheers, whistles and clapping. And so I became Mrs Lavinia Kate Hasluck.

The wedding party was driven away, with the photographer in tow, to take pictures of the bride, groom and wedding party. It had been decided to use the grounds and gardens outside the community hall where the wedding reception would be held. It was early April and the place had an array of autumn flowers in bloom, the green lawns were immaculate and the blue hills provided a splendid backdrop. We spent a good deal of time posing, trusting we would have some beautiful memories to look back on. Our drivers also had their own cameras and were clicking away alongside Tim. Not long after, wedding guests began turning up for the reception.

It had been decorated with colourful streamers, balloons and flowers. Our special table had a three-tiered wedding cake, flowers, glasses and bottles of champagne. Someone remembered we didn't drink alcohol and had put bottles of soft drink in ice buckets for us. Once someone worked the sound system out, the party got underway. There was music, dancing, food, drinks, speeches and toasts to the married couple.

Now, if you were watching a movie, at the end of the story the bride and groom get into a flash car and drive off with everyone cheering. But this was a Nyoongar celebration. I will say some of our guests stayed sober and were able to drive home themselves. Others had to have sober people drive their cars for them. Porter and I even got into the act. Me, in my Chantilly lace wedding gown, and Porter, still looking debonair in his wedding suit, made three different trips in his ute. The back was filled with drunk but happy people and we dropped them off at their respective homes. Thankfully, they lived pretty close. Then we came back and helped the other sober fullas clean up the hall. Though a bit tired, we didn't mind. Our family and friends had done us proud with all the work they had put in to make our day perfect.

Two weeks after the big event, Tim rang to say we could collect our wedding photos from the chemist. Each one of them turned out beautifully. But we noticed that photos of the wedding group taken outside the hall were not included. When we asked the chemist, we were directed to a note written on the back of one batch. It read, 'Photographs taken on cartridge number seven not available. It appears the cartridge was inserted incorrectly or the lens cap was left on.'

I reasoned that one out of fifteen rolls isn't bad. Besides, the driver had taken a few photos at that location, so we still had few memories to look back on.

HITTING THE BOOKS

Following our wedding, life in our house settled back into the usual routine. Porter and I didn't go on a honeymoon because we'd been living together as a couple for nearly seven years. It would have been nice to get away, but it wasn't a priority at that time.

However, being married meant there were a few changes to our income. I was now an official dependent of Porter's, but I still got family payments for Shane and Gary, who was back living with us on a full-time basis. Alison, who had left school by now, was working with a theatre company. She and Patrick had major roles and she spent most of her time at rehearsals with that crew. All three of them paid me board. Dad continued to contribute to the household too. Rodney had moved back to Pinjarra which made it a bit easier. We managed okay, until there was a downturn in work for Porter and he could only get part-time work. Money became pretty tight.

So in 1987, I decided to go back to do some study. It meant I would get an adult education allowance from the government and that would definitely help our household budget. My sister-in-law, Vida, told me about a course being offered where she worked at TAFE in West Perth. She was the coordinator of the unit helping Aboriginal students with their studies and any administration issues they may have had. Vida advised I could enrol that week and begin in early July.

In early May, Alison asked if we would give permission for her to travel to Europe. The theatre company they were working for had been invited to go to England for a series of performances. Patrick's uncle had written the play and there were other Nyoongar actors involved in the production. I knew most of them and knew they would look after my girl, so I gave my approval. I knew in my heart she would be alright, and it was too good an opportunity to miss. After all, she would only be gone for four weeks. That knowledge didn't stop me from crying when the big jet took off and I prayed every day she would be safe.

Apart from giving consent, we didn't have to worry about anything. The theatre company had organised it all. They had taken care of flights, passports and accommodation. All Alison had to do was turn up at the airport and get on her flight.

Back then, our house didn't have a landline. So in order to keep in touch with Alison, we went to Vida's place, made a call to England and paid her for the cost of the phone call. I was so glad to hear my daughter's voice and know she was doing okay.

On the day of their return we got to the airport early. We watched as one by one all the Nyoongars disembarked. I guarantee that when each and every one of them, Alison included, reached those of us waiting, there were tears in their eyes. One of them even got down on their knees and kissed the ground they were so happy to be back home.

In the first week in July, having completed all my enrolment and other administration forms, I began the Welfare Studies course. I had to travel from Armadale to Subiaco and that was a bit of a challenge sometimes

The course itself was very interesting and with a lot of other Nyoongar students attending, I felt right at home. Vida was a tremendous help with everything. She gave us advice, direction and counselling if it was needed. I was given a few prior learning credits from my time at teachers college and the secretarial course I had completed. This course was teaching me how to look at the circumstances of my life in a whole new way.

When I was a young mother, and being Nyoongar, decisions had always been made for me and about me. But times were changing. Now I was being taught new practical skills as well as learning about government policies and processes that I could use to help other Aboriginal people.

Results of my first round of assessments showed I was getting good marks. I participated fully in all the subjects. I particularly liked the practical components, like problem solving, how to access services and the importance of trust between client and facilitator.

With one particular problem-solving activity, the students were put into two groups. The first group of fifteen people formed a very tight circle, pressing one body against the next. Our group had to try and break into the centre. The activity was taking place outside.

We attempted everything – pulling, pushing and actually trying to trip their members. Some members of our group even resorted to bribery. Nothing worked. They were too strong and linked together too tightly.

An idea came to me and I asked the lecturer, 'Can we use any means possible?'

Her response was, 'As long as it doesn't cause any harm to anyone.'

While looking at the members of the other group, I noticed their biggest man was Big Travis. He was a Nyoongar bloke and, on this day, he was wearing tracksuit pants. We re-grouped and I whispered my plan on how we could get through their human barrier. They reluctantly agreed, so our group formed a single file line and began walking around the circle. When Walter, our group's big bloke, drew level with Big Travis, he turned and pulled Big Travis' tracksuit down. Big Travis let go of the person in front of him and in his haste to pull his trackies up, he stumbled forward.

When he went down, he took three or four others with him. A gap had opened up and our team was jumping around and cheering. We had broken through. So our team casually stepped over them as they lay there on the lawn. Walter immediately apologised to Big Travis and dobbed me in straight away.

Big Travis didn't talk to me for a few days. The next week though, he came over to our group and told Walter the reason why he had crumbled so quickly. On the day we did the 'breaking into the circle' session, Big Travis had left home in a hurry and had not put any jocks on. So when Walter pulled his trackies down, he went with them.

I completed that first semester with really good results. Financially, we were still having to budget very carefully to make ends meet. Like most other Nyoongar families we knew, we were living from one payday to the next. Every time I got paid, I shouted myself a few Scratch'n'Win lottery tickets from the nearest newsagent.

One day I was on my way home from Subiaco, but instead of going straight home I pulled into Rick's office. Jason Junior and Aimon were training with all the other dancers for a very important performance. I was hoping to talk to Rick because there was mention of those two going on an international trip and I wanted to ask him about it.

Outside Rick's office I could see a small newsagent just up the street, so I decided to buy a couple of Scratch'n'Win lottery tickets and do those while waiting to talk to Rick. It wasn't my payday so I only purchased three of the two-dollar tickets. I scratched them and two were winners. I only won about eight dollars in all. Back then, if your ticket was a winner, you could fill in your details on the back of it and go into a second chance daily lottery draw. That draw was televised and you could win fifty thousand dollars. I put my name on the back and with a quick word to the old spirits, I dropped my tickets into the barrel. I had to hurry because my sons had finished up and we could get a ride home with one of the other performers.

A week later we got word that Jason Junior and Aimon had been chosen to go to Germany to take part in presenting Australian Aboriginal dance and culture at a world expo. Thanks to Rick and those young blokes working with him, our Nyoongar culture was now going to be showcased to the world. Everyone was excited as they got their passports and other papers ready for their first big trip. I was apprehensive about them going to the other side of the world but, as with Alison a few months earlier, it was an opportunity of a lifetime. These young sons of mine had chosen to promote their Nyoongar culture, language and dance over a possible career in Aussie Rules football. I was so proud of them.

The night before they were due to fly out, we had a going-away party for them. A few uncles and aunts turned up, but it was mainly their young relatives and friends. Rather than have everyone travel home late, we said they could sleep at our place and go home in the morning. Mattresses and sleeping bags were put on the floor in the lounge room for the young blokes, and the girls set up sleeping areas in Alison's room. We had an early start the next day, so everything closed down by ten-thirty that night. We could hear loud whispering and laughter from the girl's room, but by midnight it was all quiet.

Early next day I was woken by loud banging on our front door. Checking the time, I realised it was only five o'clock. Stepping over my sons, who were lying on the lounge room floor, I partially opened our front door to peep out. Next moment, I was roughly pushed backward, causing me to fall back on a chair right near the door. A burly policeman stepped in and began shouting questions at me as I lay there. Two more policemen came through the door behind him. Porter and Dad, woken by the noise, came to see what was happening.

As soon as the police saw my big husband, they pulled their guns. Luckily, he stood still. Even Dad didn't make a move. With a smirk on his face, one of the cops said, 'Look Sarge, wall-to-wall blacks. I never seen so many niggers in one place.'

Although very upset and hurt by my fall, I managed to get to my feet. I was close to tears, but I asked them, 'What the fuck do yous want?'

The one they called Sarge told me to watch my language. He said, 'We looking for Jake Wilson and his brother. They gave this as their home address. Are they here?'

Porter said in a loud voice that we didn't even know any Wilsons. We had only just moved into this place a few months ago. Still, the police went through and pulled the blankets off those young people still laying on the floor.

Suddenly Alison, dressed only in her pyjamas, came down the hallway shouting and swearing at two munartj who had come through the back door and had smashed their way into her room. Some of the girls had been asleep in only their undies, and were shocked when the blankets were pulled off them. After a search of the room, those two cops had come down to the lounge. All her friends had followed Alison down the hallway, and were now shouting at them as well, calling them perverts. Feeling angry but still trying to keep my cool, I challenged the sergeant about doing their homework before they raided innocent people's homes. I told them to check with State Housing, if they could read, and they might find out who was living at what address.

The Sarge turned and walked out. No apology. Nothing. In all, there were eight uniformed policemen who took part in that dawn raid on us. Thank God no one was shot. I was badly bruised and I put in a formal report to the Aboriginal Legal Aid Service.

They made some inquiries, but nothing came of it. There was no record of the raid, and no information forthcoming from the police department. To them, it never happened. My bruises told another story.

Anyway, Jason, Aimon and the other performers managed to get to the airport on time. The airport was crowded with Nyoongars who had come to see them off because to the families of the dancers it was a big event. There was a lot of tissues put to good use that day. I asked God to look after my sons, Rick and everyone who flew out. I had already spoken to our old spirits asking for their protection even before I left home.

When they finally stepped off the plane almost a month later, I was the happiest mother in the whole world. My three oldest kids had travelled to the other side of the planet. I was overjoyed they had made it back to Nyoongar country.

LUCKY BREAK

A few weeks later, Dad received a letter from his brother Trev in Nullagine. He invited him to go up there for Christmas. Dad asked Porter and me if we could take him. It meant we would leave in the middle of December. The whole idea posed a real challenge because even though Porter was now working regularly, money was still an issue and I wasn't sure how we were going to manage it.

Still, I made plans so we could all go with Dad. If we could buy bulk food and set up camp and cook a meal or two during the trip, it would save money. Then we would only need to buy fuel to get up there and back. Tim said we could use his big four-wheel drive and he would look after Porter's red ute at his place.

I had never been past Carnarvon, which is about 890 kilometres north of Perth, right on the west coast, so for me it would be covering new territory. This journey would take us inland, travelling through Meekatharra, which was about 750 kilometres north of Perth, and I was really looking forward to going. We'd all pinched our pennies and hoped we would have enough to travel up there and back.

Then one day, when Dad and I had finished cleaning up after lunch, we got visitors. It was Porter's brother Pete and his wife, Pauline. When they came inside, I could see Pete was excited about something. After saying hello to Dad, he asked if I had watched the second-chance lottery draw that morning. When I said no, he yelled, 'You won the fifty thousand dollars! They called your name out right there on the television. Lavinia Hasluck. You're the winner, sis.'

For a minute, I could not believe him. He had been known to play tricks on people in the past. But then Pauline said, 'Lavinia, true as my kids, you won the fifty thousand. We came over as soon as we finished watching the draw.'

Both Dad and I stood there in the kitchen with our mouths open.

Pete asked where Porter was and I told him he was working just up the road at his boss's place. We decided to go to the nearest phone box and ring him. We knew he wouldn't leave work unless it was an emergency, so I told him Pete was at our house, drunk and making trouble. I was going to call the cops.

Porter said, 'That stupid bastard. Look mate, I'll be there in a few minutes. Don't call the cops, I'll take him back to his place. That bloody idiot.'

We heard the ute roaring down the street heading for our place. When he pulled up, Porter got out and rushed into the house. By this time, we were sitting around the kitchen table having a cuppa. When Porter walked in he said, 'What the fuck is going on here then, Lavinia?'

Pete said, 'Porter, Lavinia just won fifty thousand dollars. We saw it on TV, brother. You fullas can pick it up today.'

Porter just stared at his brother. Then Pete said, 'Me and Pauline could take you in to pick it up if you want. We still got a bit of time, but we have to go to Subiaco, so we should move soon.' Then he smiled, and with a wink at me and Dad, he said, 'It will cost you though, Port.'

Dad said he would stay and wait for Shane and Gary to get home. It didn't take long for us to get into Subiaco and even less time to establish my identity. I had to give my account details and they said it would be in my bank the next day. Having settled all that, we returned home to celebrate. Dad shouted a few beers for himself and Pete, plus some cool drinks for the rest of us. It was Porter's payday the following day and true to his promise, he gave Pete two hundred dollars for taking us into Subiaco.

I found it difficult to sleep that night. All my life I had wanted to buy my own home. Could it finally happen? We had previously applied to State Housing to purchase the house in Armadale because we had put a lot of time, energy and money into making it a decent place to live. They had knocked us back twice. I couldn't believe it when three days after the win, a Nyoongar bloke from State Housing sent us a letter saying we could now purchase that home. The old Nyoongar grapevine was obviously still working well. Porter wanted to ring and tell them to stick their offer where the sun didn't shine.

As Dad pointed out to him, 'There's no point in doing that, bloke. If you and Lavinia buy your own home, you two won't ever need that lot again. Just go forward.'

Winning that money eased so many of my financial worries and I put it to good use.

I paid off all our debts, gave some money to Porter's mum and to our own young ones, and then promised Dad we could definitely take him to Nullagine. I also set aside half of my winnings as a deposit on a house, though I didn't have a clue how to go about it. Lucy said we should contact a real estate agent and get them to help us.

So we started the ball rolling. Along with the twenty-five thousand dollar deposit, we were able to get a loan from the Aboriginal and Torres Strait Islander Commission's Aboriginal Housing Program. It was a new federal government department set up to help Aboriginal people buy their own homes.

I left the decision of which house to buy up to Porter. Being a qualified plumber – in fact we were told that he was the first qualified Aboriginal plumber in Australia – and working in the building industry, I relied on his judgement to get us the best place possible. He chose a modest three-bedroom, double brick and tile home, within a very short distance of the railway station. We didn't need a bigger house because Jason Junior had moved out and was living with his girlfriend and Alison had moved in with Patrick. Gary had gone back to Pinjarra to be with his mum. So that left only me, Porter, Dad, Shane and Aimon.

The real estate agent advised that being so close to Christmas and with some final details still to settle, we would have to wait until after the New Year before we could move in. Considering we were going to Nullagine next week, we would to be back in plenty of time to pack up everything and move into our new home.

CHRISTMAS AT NULLAGINE

The sun wasn't even up when we got underway heading for Nullagine. Porter and I were joined by Dad, my brother Clem, Shane, and my nephew Randall in the four-wheel drive. My brother Edwin was driving his own car and he had Aimon and a few other young blokes with him for company. Edwin planned to visit some of our relatives who were living in Derby at the time. He had never been that way before and wanted to catch up with them for Christmas. They had told him there was some good fishing to be done off the Derby jetty, so he decided to follow us to Nullagine, then head on to Derby.

Once we got out of the metropolitan area, the countryside was awesome. I thanked God for giving me vision. All the golden native Christmas trees – the moordgah – were in full bloom. These contrasted with the white paperbark flowers in the gullies and the deep crimson of the early flowering red gum trees. There was not a cloud in the sky and that beautiful blue only stopped when it was met with huge paddocks of pale yellow, filled with wheat, barley and other grains ready to be harvested. We soon left Nyoongar country, and mallee and maarm bari trees and thick patches of native shrubs took over as we followed the highway north through Yamatji land.

It was decided we would camp just outside Meekatharra. Everyone was tired so we pulled over, parked about a hundred metres from the road and set up camp for the night. Porter and I climbed up to the top of the four-wheel drive and made our bed. There was enough room down the other end for Shane and Randall to join us. Dad and Clem slept in the back of the vehicle, and Edwin and those in the other car pitched a tent. I knew my brothers were asleep because they would have put pigs to shame with their loud snoring, followed by a little snort every now and then.

I don't know how long I had been asleep, but I was woken by someone shaking my shoulder. It was a bright, moonlit night and I could see there was only Shane, Randall, Porter and I on the top of our vehicle. They were all fast asleep. At that height, I couldn't see anyone else near me. In the silence of the night I lay there for about *five minutes*.

Suddenly I heard a whistling sound overhead, coming towards us from the north. It was moving fast. As it got closer, I saw a blue light pass right over those of us on the roof, like an x-ray. I nearly shit myself. Feeling really scared, I shook Porter awake. Then we heard Dad say, 'It's okay, Lavinia. It's my lot, and they're only checking us out. Making sure we are alright.'

I didn't question Dad and I certainly didn't ask him who 'they' were. I just knew that my guardian spirit had woken me up and warned me that 'they' were coming.

The next morning we pulled into Meekatharra. We didn't visit my cousins who were living in town. We planned to do that on the way back. Instead we refuelled, bought some breakfast and headed out. There was still a long way to go. Nearly a hundred kilometres north of Meekatharra, Dad asked Porter to slow down and check something. He pointed out a sign off to the left. Yarlarweelor Station. He told us back in the day he used to work for the station manager. In fact, both he and Mum stayed there for quite a while. He said for their first baby, Janie, Mum had travelled back to Moore River Native Settlement to give birth. However, Lucy was actually born in Meekatharra. While he was telling us that yarn, he got a faraway look on his face as if it had only happened yesterday.

From then on, all along the road to Nullagine, Dad would tell us stories of the time he had travelled along the Great Northern Highway. He even recalled when he first came back to his Mulbpa country after being taken away over fifty years before and the roads were all gravel.

We'd rigged makeshift curtains to keep out the hot sunlight and that certainly helped. Luckily, when we were on the move, it created a breeze which would flow into the cabin, and with every window wide open, it was quite comfortable. But the minute the motor was switched off, the heat stormed in.

We arrived at the Capricorn Roadhouse and truck stop around lunchtime, 350 kilometres on from Meekatharra. It was a stinking hot day by now and everyone was glad to have a break.

After a feed and some cool drinks we got underway again. At the turn-off to Nullagine we saw two blokes hitchhiking. Dad said they must be Mulbpa and asked if we could give them a ride. We pulled up and, after a word or two, we made a few adjustments and I got out of the front seat and joined Dad, Clem and the boys in the back of the four-wheel drive.

After a quick word or two, telling Dad they were heading to Nullagine, they climbed into the front seat. They scoffed down the food and cold drinks Dad offered them. Poor fullas must have been out in the hot sun for quite a while. We would have travelled only twenty kilometres before they started nodding off. The one nearest the door went fast asleep but the one sitting nearest to Porter was definitely fighting it. Clem said he must have been worried we were going to take them somewhere else, not to Nullagine

Late in the afternoon we reached Nullagine. It was good to see some houses. We had been travelling for hours and the only buildings we saw in that time were cattle stations in the distance. Mind you, the Pilbara countryside is very beautiful with its high, iron ore–laden hills and dry river beds lined with white gum trees. But as Dad often told us, 'Beautiful, yes, but just as deadly.' He reminded us that years ago his mum had died of thirst. She and two other women were walking back to Hillside Station when they ran out of water. They didn't make it back.

Nullagine was a very small place with a pub called the Conglomerate, a garage which doubled as the town store, a police station and a caravan park. There was also a primary school and a nursing outpost. Within the town boundaries there were several houses where wadjerlars lived and a local Aboriginal community. It reminded me of the reserve in Pinjarra, built by the government to house people. Like those homes, they were all built of the same materials and located fairly close together.

We pulled up just across the road from the pub and adjacent to a park. The two hitchhikers got out and after thanking Dad and Porter, they headed south through the park. Dad and Clem walked across to the pub to get some information about where his brother, Uncle Trev, might be. He'd written Dad a month ago, plus he was a dogger – a bloke who killed dingoes for their pelts – and a prospector. Not one to stay in town for too long, he could be anywhere.

They'd been in there a few minutes when I decided to buy a few bottles of cool drink for everyone. I walked through the door where Dad and Clem had entered. They were just coming out and as they passed me, I could see Clem had a few cans with him. I was standing at the bar waiting to be served when the barman came over and told me I had to go around the other side of the pub, to a second bar. When I asked him why, he pointed to a sign above the bar. In bold letters it read 'Black People Only at this Bar'.

I said to him, 'But my dad and brother were just in this bar and they'd been served.'

He said, 'Too bad, lady, I can't help you. You gotta be served in the Whites Only bar.' I was shocked. This was in the late 1980s! Feeling disgusted, I turned and walked out.

While he was in the pub, Dad found out from the barman that Uncle Trev was in Marble Bar, another ninety kilometres further on. We settled back in the vehicle for the final leg of our journey. It didn't go at all to plan.

About halfway to Marble Bar, the radiator overheated. There was no way the blokes could fix it out on the road, so it was decided that Edwin would tow us the rest of the way. We pulled into the first garage on the way into Marble Bar and the mechanic on duty did a really good job of fixing the problem. It didn't take him very long and after we told him we'd travelled up to have Christmas with Uncle Trev, he only charged us fifty dollars and the promise of a beer to get it back on the road. Once that was done, Edwin set out with Shane and Randall for Derby. Their destination was a further 745 kilometres north and it would take them more than a full day's drive.

Once our vehicle was on the move again, Porter drove us into Marble Bar. The place was bigger than Nullagine. Again Dad and Clem went into the local pub, the Ironclad, to ask after Uncle Trev. They emerged some minutes later accompanied by an old bloke about Dad's age, but a bit shorter. Like Dad, he had grey hair protruding from under his weather-beaten old hat and his face looked like tanned leather. They walked over to the four-wheel drive and Dad proudly introduced us to Uncle Trev. They really looked like a pair of old cowboys and I could see the joy of catching up with each other after nearly two decades. Their gap-toothed old smiles said it all.

Once the introductions were over, Uncle Trev asked us to follow him to his daughter Nita's house. That was where he lived whenever he was in town and he had made provision for us to stay there too. Along with her husband and kids, Nita had gone to Port Hedland to pick up all the Christmas shopping, food and presents and was due back that afternoon. In the meantime, Dad and Clem had gotten into Uncle Trev's little blue Suzuki four-wheel drive and he had us follow him around Marble Bar, pointing out all the interesting places, in and around town that only the locals would know. Then they went back to the pub to have a few beers to celebrate the reunion.

It was still two days to Christmas and apart from a few cans of reduced cream, fruit and tinned pudding, I had not packed anything for that special day. I need not have worried. When Nita arrived back from shopping, it seemed she must have bought out half the stores in Port Hedland. There was heaps of food. Uncle Trev was putting half of everything in some big boxes and placing these in his vehicle. He also had two enormous eskies and these were filled with drinks. When I asked Dad what was happening, he told me and Porter, 'My brother's taking us bush. We going to have Christmas on the Nullagine River with him and his sons.'

We left around lunchtime on Christmas Eve and travelled south-east from Marble Bar. I had the privilege of driving Uncle Trev's vehicle. I was later told he never let any other female drive his pride and joy. Porter was joined by Clem, Uncle Trev's oldest son, Frank, and his daughter Andrea. Also in tow was Rolly, one of his nephews.

It was about three hours later that we pulled up and made camp. Porter and I planned to sleep in our vehicle and we were joined by Andrea. We could have made our beds near where Dad and the other men were going to sleep, but I didn't feel comfortable about doing that. As usual I followed my instincts and we stayed in the vehicle for the night. Before settling down, after supper the blokes sat around drinking beer and yarning, with Dad and his brother catching up. I jumped straight into bed, but still heard everyone laugh when Dad and Uncle Trev told the others I had mistakenly called a bush turkey a deformed emu.

Sometime during the night I woke up and felt around for the bottle of water I had earlier placed near my pillow. The night was still warm and I sat up to take a drink. The Pilbara was lit up with a full moon and outside it was so bright it almost looked like daylight. My attention was caught by movement around where the blokes had settled for the night. Bright electric blue lights were shining and spreading out over all of them as they slept. I was mesmerised. Suddenly it disappeared, vanished from my sight. This time I felt safe and this time the lights were bouncing around as if our old spirits were dancing, happy that my dad had come back to his country.

The next day we drove for another ten kilometres and came to a dry river bed, wide with soft yellow sand. There was plenty of shade from the multitude of white gum trees lining the banks. Much further along, we could see the remnants of a billabong holding mud rather than water. Uncle Trev decided we'd set up for our Christmas dinner right there.

Everyone pitched in with the food preparation. The blokes built a fire and roasted enough potatoes and pumpkin for everyone. Once they were cooked, we opened some tins of green vegies. These, along with huge slices of leg ham, were dished out for us on Uncle Trev's tin plates. We also had Christmas pudding, tin cream and a variety of tinned fruits. After eating so much, everyone found a shady spot under the trees and put a blanket on the ground to have a rest. Dad opted to lie in the back of the four-wheel drive with the windows and back door wide open so he would get the breeze that was being channelled down the riverbed towards us.

It was about six o'clock that evening before we started to move around again. Porter and I had gone for a short walk and when we returned Clem said we should check on Dad.

He didn't look good at all. When Uncle Trev came over, he said we would pack up and take him back to Marble Bar to the medical outpost.

We got there very late and took Dad straight up to see the nurse on duty. After examining him, she rang the doctor and was given instructions to get a drip into Dad's arm. Apparently he was severely dehydrated, despite all the beer he had to drink with his brother. He stayed overnight under the watchful care of the nurse and was released the next morning.

We decided to stay a few more days in and around Marble Bar to meet the rest of Uncle Trev's family before heading home.

The two old cowboys got drunk again and challenged their youngest sons out for a fight. I remember them both saying, 'C'mon you young bastards. I got my brother here now for my backstop. Give me your best shot. I'll knock you right out. Put 'em up!'

They weren't bouncing around like Mohammed Ali. It was more Jack Johnson style. Both of them were pissed and could hardly stand, but the shirts came off, showing more wrinkles than muscles on their bony old arms. When Porter and Frank finally managed to calm them down, they said, 'Those young fullas are lucky you blokes stopped us. We would have flogged them, right brother?'

On the journey home, a few unexpected things happened. Just on dark, when Porter switched on the headlights, the whole engine cut out. He checked under the bonnet and found the alternator wasn't working. He could start the engine, but the minute the lights came on it began to splutter, then cut right out. The only lights we could switch on without that happening were the parking lights. There wasn't much traffic on the road, so to get some mileage Porter continued to drive homewards. He did pull over to the side and park every time a vehicle came from the opposite direction. Once that passed, we would then move on again. Luckily the moon was still shining really bright.

We were not too far from Meekatharra when we saw a car pull out in front of us, heading in same direction. Porter decided to use those lights as a guide for us. He drove right up behind it and virtually tailgated the car. When the car in front sped up, Porter sped up. When it slowed down, our vehicle did the same. Our situation was dire, and the person in front must have thought we were lunatics, but we had to laugh when he tried to speed up and still couldn't get away from us.

Finally the car in front pulled into a big parking bay. We followed because Porter wanted to explain why we had driven so close. We noticed there was already a vehicle parked there and when the person pulled over and got out of his rig, he just about sprinted to that vehicle.

Those lot switched their headlights on, then directed a very bright spotlight right onto us.

Turned out the bloke Porter was tailgating was travelling alone and had just come back from hunting. He planned to meet his friends at that particular parking bay and give them some kangaroo meat. He said he was getting really spooked by our little lights because the week before he had seen, and been followed by, the min-min lights.

He thought they'd come back for him! And it turned out that the people who had turned the bright spotlight on us was my first cousin Jo and her husband. Once we'd sorted all that out, we ended up spending the night at my cousin Madeline's place in Meekatharra.

Next day, one of my nephews, a deadly bush mechanic, fixed the alternator and we had no problem with the headlights. We hit the road for home well into the afternoon and travelled in the cool of the night. We got all the way to New Norcia early the next morning. Then the four-wheel drive broke down again. I for one, was glad it was daylight. The yarns Mum used to tell us about New Norcia and the mission where she'd grown up was enough to scare the hell out of us.

Porter and I managed to hitch a ride to Perth and brought the red ute back. The four-wheel drive was towed to Tim's place in Belmont. There we heard the news that Edwin, Aimon, Shane and Randall had made it safely back from Derby. They'd driven down the coastal highway, which was a longer route, yet they had beaten us back by two days.

It's not exactly the best way to finish a holiday with the four-wheel drive breaking down again, but for us it was a fantastic trip. We had travelled from Mum's Nyoongar country in the South West, through Yamatji country, then on to Dad's Mulbpa country in the Pilbara. We met a whole lot of new relatives and extended family in Marble Bar, caught up with my cousins and their families in Meekatharra and even made a few new friends. We had Christmas on the Nullagine River. Most importantly, Dad had spent time with his brother in their own country.

NEW BEGINNING

In the middle of January, Porter and I picked up the keys from the real estate office and we moved into our new home. It gave us a couple of weeks to settle in before I had to go back to my studies at TAFE. I only had two semesters to go before I graduated and I wanted to get the best marks I possibly could.

Shane and Gary were now at an age where they could decide if they wanted to continue with school. Jason Junior and his girlfriend, April, were expecting their first baby. And Alison and Patrick were due to become parents around the same time. Aimon gravitated between our place and his workmates' homes. Both he and Jason were still working with their Uncle Rick.

Porter and I became grandparents right near the end of January. Jason and April had a beautiful baby girl, Jean. She had a lot of jet-black hair that fell in ringlets. Her Nyoongar name was Koomool, the possum. Then three weeks later Alison and Patrick gave us another beautiful granddaughter, Demi. My dad gave her a name, Mardignu, meaning sweetheart. Both girls brought me a joy that I couldn't explain. It was a combination of love and absolute awe. Here were my two granddaughters, the beginning of our family's next generation. It did cross my mind that at thirty-eight I was a bit young to be a Nanna, but as Jason pointed out, 'Mum, you had me when you were sixteen, I'm a dad at twenty-one and Alison is a mum at eighteen. And Aimon and Shane haven't even started yet.

Plus look at it this way, your rank in the family just got higher.'

So I began my last year of study as a young grandmother. Again I got good marks and I was offered a chance to earn some extra money tutoring other Nyoongar students who were just coming into the course. I agreed and organised my time so I could help them without impacting too much on my own studies. Then, when Vida went on leave, I was given the opportunity to become acting coordinator for the Aboriginal unit, helping all the students with their administration and study issues.

I welcomed the added responsibility and I found it challenging because during that time I had to attend weekly meetings with other staff yet still maintain my student status when attending lectures. I was glad when Vida returned, but I had learned a lot. Especially about time management.

I still had four months to complete my TAFE studies, and as we would be graduating soon, one of the assignments for final year students involved finding employment where we would put our skills to good use. We had to look for five jobs advertised in the newspapers, research what was involved in the work and the qualifications required for each one. Then we had to apply for them. I actually thought a few of those I chose were way out of my league, but I sent them in anyway. I completed that assignment and thought no more about it. At the very least I would graduate.

Porter still didn't have full-time work and it was around that time we considered going into business for ourselves. I would do the administration side of it and he would put his trade skills to good use. So we put together an initial business plan for an Aboriginal plumbing company. As part of that, we had to make sure we would get work contracts before we applied for any type of funding, either through a government initiative or private loan.

There were quite a few Nyoongar organisations in the South

West and we arranged to visit them. We wanted to promote our idea and ask if they would hire us once we got it up and running. The response to our research was very promising. It cost us a lot in fuel and time, and we travelled all around the South West, and even the Goldfields region, promoting our idea. On the days when I couldn't go, Porter had his cousin Charlie accompany him on the long road trips. He named our proposed business venture the Ab-Trades Plumbing Company.

Late in August a letter arrived at our place and I showed it to Porter. It was from one of the agencies where I had applied for a job. It advised I had been shortlisted for the position and was inviting me in for an interview. I read it several times because it was one of those jobs that I considered a bit beyond my reach.

The position on offer was the State Co-ordinator for Women's Issues and it was at an administrative officer's level 7 job in the Federal Department of Aboriginal Affairs. With an attitude of 'in for a penny, in for a pound', I rang and arranged an appointment with them.

The interview was a daunting exercise. First, I had to travel thirteen storeys in a lift to get to the office and that's not easy for someone who suffers from mild vertigo in tall buildings. I then had to face three people sitting behind a huge desk firing all sorts of questions at me.

Talk about feeling like a target on a rifle range. I answered all their questions and told them a bit about myself. I made sure to mention that I had one final practical assessment to complete my studies. Still reeling a bit from the interview, when I got downstairs, I rang Porter and told him how it went. I wasn't very optimistic about my chances, but he wished me good luck anyway.

Ten days later, I handed Porter another letter to read. I had been offered the job and they asked if I would be able to start in two weeks' time. This position would finally give me financial security. I showed the letter to my children and I was congratulated by each and every one of them. Dad was very pleased for me too. He said, 'Nothing wrong with working for the government. I did it for forty years on the Public Works Department in Pinjarra. It got me lot of what I wanted, my girl, and helped me and your mum keep food on the table for the lot of you.'

In order to take up the offer as State Coordinator for Women's Issues with the Department of Aboriginal Affairs, I had to do one last exam at TAFE and complete my final three-month placement. Then I would be fully qualified. It was arranged through the lecturers that my first three months in my new job would also count as my final TAFE placement. I would be on a probationary period at the department for those three months anyway, to see if I was suitable to continue in the position.

When I brought home my first pay packet, I felt like I had hit the jackpot. Previously we had been living on a combination of social security benefits, family payments for Shane and Gary, my student allowance and Porter's part-time work. Now I earned nearly triple that amount.

We had managed before because I had budgeted carefully. So, when I asked my kids what was I going to do with all this extra money their collective response was, 'Don't worry, give it to us, we'll spend it for you, Mum.'

The first thing I did arrange was for our mortgage repayments to be taken directly out of my wages. I really did want to keep my home that I had waited so long to own.

The probationary three months flew by, and I became a permanent member of staff.

WOMEN'S BUSINESS

My role as State Coordinator for Women's Issues turned out to be a real challenge.

There were a few Nyoongars working there and had been doing so for a while. They were very helpful when I was settling in, telling me all about the unofficial hierarchy and office politics.

There were seven regional offices throughout the state and my role was to liaise with the Regional Women's Officer in each area. Geographically, it ranged from the remote regions in the east and north, to the more populated centres throughout the Mid West and South West.

When I first went to visit the two northern regional offices in Derby and Kununurra, they took me out to meet with local Aboriginal community women's groups in the areas. They didn't question whether I was Aboriginal or not, they just asked, 'Who your mob and where they come from?'

After I told them a bit about my family connections, the older women in the group didn't say much. But they did nod, as if giving permission for the younger spokeswomen to work with me.

A couple of times when I had to stay over a weekend, I was invited to go bush with them. Being a Nyoongar woman, I considered it a privilege and a sign that I was accepted by the group. I always gave thanks to my dear mother who had taught me about our Nyoongar protocols and how to conduct myself when I was a visitor in someone else's country. It certainly stood me in good stead.

At the women's meetings right throughout the state, we discussed a range of concerns, including economic development, housing, education, funding and projects they were interested in getting off the ground. One of the key problems was family violence and how to cope with the growing number of violent incidents perpetrated against our women. It seemed as if somebody was getting bashed and hospitalised every week with no recourse.

One good thing was that after each visit to the communities, I had to provide a report to our state manager. This information would later be included in a national report on Aboriginal women's issues and it was hoped the powers that be would do something about it.

Within the first month of being in the role, I was invited to Canberra to meet with the National Coordinator for Aboriginal Women's Issues. Ellen was Aboriginal and originally from South Australia. She met me at the airport in Canberra and I told her I was chuffed to be flying first class. When I had travelled to Adelaide to compete in the national Aboriginal netball championships, I was seated in economy class along with all my team mates. For me, being in first class was a big deal because on this flight I had more leg room and was treated like a VIP.

Before going to head office, Ellen took me for a mini tour of our national capital. It was impressive. But I pondered the fact that so many of the recent laws and policies affecting our people had been sanctioned from this place. I wondered if any of those rule-makers or their predecessors had ever experienced any of the pain and suffering that had been inflicted on our people since colonisation.

Although it was a short visit to introduce me to the national office staff, I gained a lot of information from Ellen about what was expected of me as the State Coordinator for Women's Issues. Over the next year, we met a few times at conferences and workshops. We spoke regularly over the phone and she gave me good advice on how to effectively operate the state Aboriginal women's program within the confines of the federal government's direction. It was a pleasure to work with her and she became my long-distance mentor.

At home, Porter was kept busy setting up his plumbing business. With support and advice from a number of state and federal training bodies, it was decided that instead of only launching an Aboriginal plumbing company, he should create an Aboriginal building company. We had already done a lot of consultation across the state with Aboriginal community groups the previous two years, seeking their support for the plumbing venture. It was a simple transition to expand it to include other trades.

So I registered Ab-Trades – short for Aboriginal Tradesmen – as a business. The only catch was, instead of being a private company, and in order to get Aboriginal government funding, we had to become an incorporated body. This meant we had to have an elected governing committee. The Ab-Trades Plumbing Company was the first all-Aboriginal building company in Western Australia and it operated under the commercial name as the Yawony Building Company. Porter had created the name by using the first two letters of Yamatji, Wongi and Nyoongar.

The concept of an Aboriginal building company was a massive undertaking. It consisted of three components: administration, construction and training. After much consultation, meetings and a kick start with government funding, Porter and his crew were fortunate enough to secure their first contract building a house in Yanchep. It took a year, and once that was completed, they received a contract to build seven houses, an ablution block and a wiltja on the Meekatharra reserve. This took another two years to complete. As well, during that period of time, they were given smaller contracts throughout the state. Most of the tradesmen in those projects were Aboriginal people and Porter managed the actual onsite projects. It meant he was away from home quite a bit.

Luckily, I still had Dad, Aimon, Shane and Gary at home for company. Jason Junior, Alison and their little families lived nearby so I was never lonely. But I did miss Porter and was glad to catch up when we could. I remember travelling to Meekatharra and spending a week with him, living in his donga on the construction site. While he was at work I spent the day with my cousin, Madeline. *We went looking for gemstones and she showed me several special* sites near the town.

Once the Meekatharra project was finished, and before another big project was undertaken, Porter concentrated on the training component. The company had been given several smaller contracts and, in conjunction with TAFE, he used those to give young Aboriginal people the opportunity to learn about the construction industry while training on the job. The intention was for them to be given apprenticeships with other companies in the building industry once they passed muster. Everything was going great.

Then, after six years of building the business up, putting much of our own time, energy and money into the project, in a shock decision by the governing committee and its members – who actually included close family – both Porter and I were voted out.

We were blindsided. There was no way we could have predicted such an outcome. It hurt us badly. Holding almost daily post-mortems on their decision to oust us began to affect our marriage. Dad could see what was happening was doing neither of us any good. About a week later while having a cuppa with us he told us, 'Don't sit here feeling sorry for yourself and blaming each other. Do something about it.'

When Dad gave me that advice, I don't think he had in mind what I ended up doing. I said to Aimon, 'Get in the car, you're coming with me to watch my back.'

I got a baseball bat from my car boot, went to their office, took the Business Registration Certificate for Ab-Trades – that I had paid for – off the wall, then turned two desks over. Phones and computers crashed to the floor. Still a bit shocked, one of the staff members – a fairly big bloke – came in from outside and told Aimon, 'Get her out of here before we start on her.'

Before Aimon could say anything, I grabbed an axe from the back of a worker's ute. I shouted at them to bring it on, but all four staff took off down the road.

Aimon and I went back home and he told his grandfather what had happened. Dad did seem a bit shocked, but all he said was, 'You okay, my girl?'

I nodded.

'Now leave it be, and move on,' he said.

I did expect the munartj would turn up, but nobody came. No one reported me to the police so I was never charged with anything, but shortly afterwards they moved the office to a different location.

YORGA DREAMING

In 1990 the Department of Aboriginal Affairs was replaced by the Aboriginal and Torres Strait Islander Commission (ATSIC). My role was now defunct, but in its place I was given a position as a senior policy and project officer and the added responsibility of three portfolios: Women, Sport, and Social Programs. By this time I was really proficient in my job and the transition went fairly smoothly.

One real challenge I did have was to learn about the new ATSIC specific programs, which were now all computerised. That was only one of the many training programs I was obliged to attend while on the job. It certainly simplified a lot of the interaction between regional, state and commonwealth offices. Prior to this, I had done most of my communication via the phone, typewriters, faxes and internal memos. Over the first few weeks, under my breath, I swore at my brand new computer in Nyoongar and English quite a few times until I got the hang of it.

My role was never boring, and I enjoyed helping my people. At times I did put in some long hours, especially when some older Nyoongar relatives would seek information. They didn't want to travel by bus into the city, so after I knocked off, I would visit them at their home and give them the information they wanted.

During that time, I had a recurring dream over about six months. I told Porter about it. In my dreaming, I was journeying along a very rough road in a big bus. Madeline, my cousin in Meekatharra, was there sitting beside me. First we were high in the hills, nothing like the ones in our Pinjarra area where we had walked as children. No, they were so much bigger and higher. Then we were travelling along a bush track in the bus. The bus stopped and we came upon a big clearing, a tank near a windmill and some stockyards. Tall, straight, slender saplings and trees dotted the area, but I had a feeling of foreboding. Then I would wake up, happy to be in my own bed.

One day I received an invitation from Canberra to attend a women's conference in Queensland. It said I should get three nominations from each of the regional women's officers to accompany us to this national event. I passed the message on and left it to them to choose who the community women would be.

Upon arrival at the airport in Cairns, I was met by some of the WA contingent. I was surprised and pleased to see Maddie standing with the Mid West group. Organisers of the conference were also there to greet us, and once everyone from around Australia had arrived, we spent the night in town and got underway very early the next morning in a large bus. We had to leave early because as they told us, the trip would be some three hundred kilometres north-west of Cairns and the going may be slow. Of course, I sat next to Madeline because we had a lot of family news to catch up on.

We left the city and were driven up some very high hills, travelling through the Atherton Tablelands. It was some of the most spectacular country I had ever seen. Then it hit me. This was the high country I had seen in my dream! And Maddie was seated right beside me!

I could hardly wait to see if the rest of my recurring travelling dream would come true. Sure enough, towards to end of our journey we had to travel along a track overgrown with shrubs. The bus pushed on through them and we came to a big clearing, pulling up when we came to an area with tall, straight trees and saplings. A short distance away was a tank standing beside a big windmill.

But no stockyards. I thought I must be mistaken, even though everything else appeared as it did in my dream-travelling. I had an involuntary shiver and wasn't too surprised when Maddie said, 'Do you feel it too, Lavinia? Something bad happened here. It's not a good place. It's warra, sis.'

Ours was the last bus to arrive, and I saw there was nearly a hundred women already there, setting up tents and unloading their luggage. After a while, the conference organisers asked everyone to *meet at the big clearing in fifteen minutes*. After going through the program for the next few days, they asked if anyone wanted to add or say anything.

I put my hand up. Into the microphone I said, 'I don't feel comfortable here. Something bad happened here and my spirit is not happy. Where are the people who come from this area? I don't know about everyone else, but I want to know if their Elders are going to welcome us, to invite us on to their land?'

It was obvious the organisers hadn't even thought about it, but they did promise they would get someone from the Quinkan people to welcome us. Sure enough, that afternoon, shortly after lunch we were asked to gather again at the big clearing. After everyone formed a big circle and held hands, we were introduced to a group of local people. Just as they gave us their official welcome in their own language and in English, three eagles flew over the top of everyone. To me, that was very significant. My spirit soared with them.

Later that day, as we were about to settle down, a group of women came over to our tent to talk with me. They thanked me for asking for someone local to welcome us to this country. They had wanted to say it too, but did not know how for fear of offending someone. I felt very humble when they gave me a djoonah, a women's fighting stick made of very hard wood from their own country, as a gift.

There were a few hiccups. Like the tank connected to the windmill running out of water which meant we had to have a wash in the nearby river. It scared the shit out of some of us when a taipan snake skin was found on the path on one of the trips there. Apparently it had only recently shed its skin. Everyone was on red alert after that. Eventually the army was brought in to help with fresh water and other supplies. Even with those few problems, I believe our mob benefited from being there.

The day before we were due to leave, three trucks pulled up and six men got out. This conference was a women's-only event. Apart from the few male soldiers, we hadn't seen a bloke in all the days we were there. They began unloading the trucks, putting up stockyards not far from the windmill. Apparently the stockyards were in preparation for an annual rodeo which was due to get under way the following fortnight. We would be long gone by then. My dreaming hadn't let me down!

BIRRDIERS' MIA-MIA

It was a Monday and I had just returned from spending a week's holiday in Meekatharra with Porter when I received a request from head office in Canberra. I had been recommended by Ellen to attend an Executive Management for Women training course at Mount Eliza Business School on the Mornington Peninsula in Victoria. This wasn't any run of the mill training – it was an exclusive course for females at the top management level. After a brief discussion and agreement with the deputy state manager, I took up the offer.

As I was leaving his office, he said, 'I'm not certain, Lavinia, but you may be the first Aboriginal woman to do this course. Good luck.'

Two weeks later, I pulled up in a taxi outside a mansion. A castle would have been a better word to describe it. It was huge and the grounds were expansive and immaculately maintained. It was a million miles from my first home in Pinjarra with its four rooms made of timber and tin.

Inside was as impressive as the outside. Thick carpet and chandeliers featured in every common area, especially the dining area. After checking in at reception, I was shown around, then taken upstairs to my accommodation. My room was sparsely decked out with expensive looking furniture, but there was no phone and no television. There was also a small bookshelf filled with texts related to business management. It was obvious we were there to work.

In contrast, the view was fantastic. I could actually see the waters of Port Phillip Bay not too far away.

I went down to the evening meal and met a few of the other participants. I began to feel out of my depth when some women introduced themselves as the head of well-known national companies. The meal was a very formal silver service occasion. I had been to restaurants before but this was something else.

Eight pieces of cutlery sat beside the prettiest, most delicate glasses, plates and cups I had ever seen. The person seated beside me, sensed my discomfort and in a friendly voice she whispered, 'Just start at the outside and work your way in with each course.' I smiled for the first time since I got there. 'Thank you. At home we only have one of each.' I felt a whole lot better when she replied, 'That's the same at my place, too.'

After the initial culture shock, I settled down and focused on the training. I completed all that was asked of me as an individual student, with good results, and our group project received the highest score. I was really glad I did that course. I learned a whole lot about how big companies operate and wished I had done it before setting up Ab-Trades. I also learned plenty of new words. Business speak, I was told. Being there gave me a brief glimpse into how the other half – the very, very wealthy half – lived. I knew, in spite of everything that lifestyle had to offer, it would not suit this Nyoongar yorga.

KYAH DAD

In the office, my day started off with the usual round of messages and phone calls. Then I was asked to go to the deputy state manager's office. With a bit of trepidation, I knocked on his door.

'Come in.' He wasted no time in telling me the reason for the meeting. 'Good morning, Lavinia. I received a letter from Canberra yesterday. It's from the federal Attorney-General's office asking me to provide some information about you and the work you have been doing with our Aboriginal women's program. Apparently, you made quite an impression at a recent conference you attended in Sydney when you spoke with one of the keynote speakers.'

My mind went back to that day. A professor of law at the conference had been giving a spiel about how the legal system was helping Aboriginal women. I couldn't let it pass. Following his presentation, I approached him, introduced myself and said I wasn't happy with what he had said. With respect, I pointed out that the information he had presented was, in so many ways, inaccurate. It painted a false picture of what was really happening in our Aboriginal communities. His information could put our women's efforts back ten years. I told him to get his facts straight and check more recent data on the subject.

He didn't pursue the challenge then, but said he would follow it up. And now this request for information about me. For a moment

I thought I had really overstepped the mark. I guessed they thought I was out of line. Maybe I was going to be given my marching orders. After all, I was only a policy officer challenging a professor who was teaching law. What did I know?

Robert said, 'So, in response to the request I have already sent some information back. Most likely we will be hearing more about this, but don't look so worried. You've been doing a real good job.'

His words lifted a big weight off my worried shoulders as I went back to work.

A few weeks later I received a letter from the Attorney-General's office asking if I would be interested in accepting a nomination for an appointment to the federal Family Law Council. I couldn't believe it. The letter went on to say if I was to accept the nomination, my name would be put before a selection committee for consideration. As they only met once every three months, I would most likely be notified in due course, probably early next year.

I was so excited I immediately rang Porter to let him know before I formally accepted the nomination in writing. I had to pinch myself to make sure I wasn't dreaming. Over the next few days, I was still on a high. I did some research to see what I would be doing and what the position entailed. I would be part of a panel considering laws that could impact on every Australian citizen. That is, if the recommendations passed through parliament. I would be in the company of the top legal minds in this country – lawyers, barristers, family court judges and other people considered experts in their fields.

It was early the next afternoon, while I was discussing the pros and cons of the nomination with a few workmates, I got a call from the hospital where Dad had been admitted. His health had been pretty fragile over the past few weeks and he had spent a few days in hospital.

They asked if I could come in soon as possible because they had some information for me. I knocked off early, and went to see him.

Usually I came to see him straight after work each day around five o'clock in afternoon. At that time, people in the wards were always bustling about bringing meals to the patients and the nurses double-checking charts. When I got to the ward about two o'clock that afternoon, the lights were quite dim, the room quiet and Dad was half asleep. He stirred when I walked in and he seemed to brighten up when he saw me. He looked so frail, my heart went out to him.

I kissed him on the forehead and told him Porter would be in later, as soon as he knocked off work. When I asked if he'd had any visitors that day, he just shook his head. I told Dad my good news about the nomination and though his breathing was pretty shallow, he said he was proud of me.

A nurse came to check his stats and asked if I would come with her to the nurse's station. She told me Dad's condition was critical and had taken a downturn. The doctors didn't expect him to live much longer. The damage to his lungs from years of smoking tobacco was making it difficult for him to breathe and his other organs were shutting down. There was nothing anyone could do.

I knew Dad was sick, but I was shocked. I thought this stint in hospital would be like the other times he was admitted, then got better and came home. I immediately tried to contact family members using the hospital phone, to no avail. I couldn't reach anyone.

Before going back into the ward, I washed the tears from my face. I had to be strong for him. This wasn't about me, it was about Dad, but it hurt so much to know I was going to lose him. Once back at his bedside, I sat in silence for a long time, holding his hand while he drifted in and out of sleep. The only sound I heard was the quiet humming of the air conditioner and the machines keeping Dad alive. Every time he woke up, he would smile and we'd yarn and swap stories some more, even though his breathing was beginning to be more laboured. Despite his body being very weak, his mind was still very clear.

When Porter turned up a few hours later, Dad perked up a bit. We started talking about horseracing and I remember Dad told him I couldn't pick my nose let alone pick a winner. We yarned a bit more and Dad asked if Porter would go and pick Verna up. He said he wanted to see her.

'She's the nurse in the family, and she will explain to me what is happening, what these doctors are going on about.'

After Porter had left, Dad and I talked some more. He was especially worried about his youngest son, Clem. I tried to assure him that Clem would be fine. We would all be fine. I reminded him that he and Mum had done a mighty job and had reared us up to be strong people, teaching us about how to survive in this tough world and teaching us right from wrong in both the Nyoongar and wadjerlar ways.

All the while, I sat there holding his wrinkled old hands in mine, and every now and then stroked his weather-beaten forehead. When the nurse came in, Dad looked right at me. I could see he was fighting to stay.

With a very heavy heart I whispered to him, 'I love you, my Dad. All your family gunna be right. You've earned your rest and Mum is waiting for you.'

He then closed his eyes. I looked at the nurse, but she just shook her head.

Verna and Porter came bursting into the room. She rushed over and started talking to Dad, but there was no response. The nurse looked at the three of us and simply said, 'I'm sorry.'

We three sat there for hours. Nobody rushed us to leave the ward. Although very sad, I took comfort knowing Dad was no longer in any pain, and he was now with Mum. I sat there still holding his hand, remembering all the time I had spent with him. Times when he piggy-backed me from the movies when I was only five and too tired to walk the mile home. As an adult, how he gave me a home whenever I needed it – no questions asked. Being there with Mum when I went into labour for my first-born child. Standing on the side cheering me on when I played state netball. Taking us to meet our Palyku family in Nullagine.

Dad and Mum had been my towers of strength throughout my life and I was so honoured that he came and lived the last fifteen years of his life with me, Porter and our family, never mind we shifted homes three times. His loyalty as a father to me never faltered. His advice always had my best interests at heart. I was so proud to be his daughter and I know God truly blessed me when He chose him to be my father. Later, as we left the hospital, I made a silent promise. Anything I achieved in the future would be in honour of Mum and Dad.

EPILOGUE

I was so lost in my memories for a moment all of us around the campfire just sat in silence. A sudden gust of cold wind brought everyone back to the present and we drew our blankets closer around us. My oldest granddaughter, Jean, stood up and, without saying a word, came over and put her arms around me to give me strength. Very quietly, I told her I was alright. Then out loud I said, 'Hey, look at the time. I've been talking for hours. I have to get some sleep. It's alright for you good-looking lot. If I don't get to sleep soon, I might wake up wrinkly. I'll tell you more tomorrow night. Goodnight. Love you lot.'

I stood up and made my way to the four-wheel drive. My recollections had worn me right out. I climbed into the back of the four-wheel drive and without disturbing anyone else, I lay down to rest. By now the night had become really very cold, so I pulled the warm blanket closer around my body. I gave my soft pillow a few punches, put my head on it and closed my tired eyes. I was soon fast asleep.

I awoke from my sleep to the smell of jarrah wood smoke and cooked bacon wafting through the window. It took me back to my childhood and waking up to the smell of breakfast being cooked on the open fire and the sound of my Mum bustling around in our kitchen at the old place. She always had a big pot of porridge for us kids and once it was dished out, we added milk, butter and a sprinkle of sugar. Most days there was also bacon and eggs or something savoury for Dad.

For a minute or two, I just lay there taking in the aroma, anticipating how that bacon was going to taste with fried eggs and toast cooked over an open fire. And my morning kick-starter of course – my mug of tea.

I reached out to wake Porter, but his side of the bed was empty. Obviously he'd risen earlier and climbed out of the vehicle without waking me. That's quite a feat for a big bloke. I must have been really, really tired from all the yarning with my grandchildren the night before. Right now I was hungry and my kobbul was telling me that food was definitely calling my name.

I rummaged around, found my shoes and stood up outside to greet my day. I was overawed by the beauty of the place. From here, I could see right down the river. The morning was still and the sky was perfectly clear. The calm water reflected the azure blue, as if a giant, long mirror had been laid out before us, extending to the horizon and lined perfectly with green shrubs and eucalyptus trees. I gave a quiet 'Thank you, God' for giving me my sight to witness such beauty.

'Good morning, Nan. Bit of a sleepyhead this morning, are we?' That was the cheeky sound of my grandson Bruce.

Porter chimed in with, 'Did you sleep well, mate? You came to bed pretty late. Last I heard, you was telling those young fullas stories from old Pinjarra days. They even asked me if I owned a bright red V8 ute. Anyway, my dear, over there is a dish with fresh water to wash your hands and face. Oh, and see that little building over yonder? I know all you girls went bush last night, but that's actually the toilet, if you need it.'

Jean came over and said she would come company with me.

As we were walking back to the others, she asked me, 'Nan,

are you going to finish telling us about your life today? I found it awesome what you told us. You know, it did take me a long while to get to sleep after that. You have been through so much. We never knew you went through that much shit. You always seem so positive and encouraging to us. I got angry too, Nan, about how you and all our mob were treated.'

We walked in silence for a little while before she said, 'Nan, what happened with the nomination you mentioned last night?'

'It ended up pretty good actually. I became the first Aboriginal person to be appointed to the federal Family Law Council, helping to make laws that could affect every Australian in the country, black and white.'

I smiled at her look of surprise. Yes, I certainly had come a long way since my humble beginnings as a young Nyoongar girl from Pinjarra.

AUTHOR'S NOTE

The reason I began writing this story was for my children and grandchildren. I wanted to share with them how it was for me, a young Nyoongar girl, growing up in a small country town in the 1950s. I wanted them to know I had been brought up tough, though loved and cared for by Mum and Dad.

My journey has been a long one, and it is important that my family know my story. They will realise there is more to me than the Mum and Nanna they see now. They can read for themselves about the trials and tribulations I faced, as well as the serendipitous and triumphant moments I was fortunate enough to experience. It wasn't always an easy ride. But it might help them understand how – through the grace of God, my culture and the old spirits, my mum and dad, and a whole lot of perseverance and luck – I managed to survive and even come out on top.

I also wanted to pass on the stories I had been told by my parents and other Elders – those who lived through some traumatic times, such as the forced removal of Aboriginal children from their parents; the attempted decimation of our language and culture; the dual role of the police as protectors of Aborigines and enforcers of law and government policy, which left our people powerless.

Stories like mine can educate our young people, and future generations, not only about the struggles Nyoongars faced, but the strength we found to overcome so much adversity. It shows that we Aboriginal people should be proud that we have survived the onslaught of colonial invasion. How we have faced racism in all its ugly forms and – almost as bad – the paternalistic attitude of other Australians treating us as if we were unable to make decisions for ourselves.

Parts of my story may surprise and even shock some readers. But it will be an insight into the life of an Aboriginal girl growing up in an era of white domination, change and what it is like to be knocked down, but to always get back up.

My story is not unique. This is the story of just one moorditj yorga – though there are many like me, growing from childhood through to being a mother and grandmother, always moving between two cultures and grabbing opportunities with both hands and making the most of them. Facing so many challenges but remaining steadfast in her belief in God and her Nyoongar culture and spirituality.

NYOONGAR GLOSSARY

The Nyoongar people have lived in the south-west of Western Australia for more than 45,000 years. The written form of our language is drawn from an oral tradition and contains many dialects and spellings. The spellings in this glossary come from my mother's culture and reflect the pronunciations of the Binjarib Nyoongar people.

Ab-Trades	The name created by Nyoongar man Athol P. Hansen. The name for a group of Aboriginal tradesmen. Later became a registered business company.
birrdier	Boss, head person, an Elder; can be male or female.
bilyah	river
Binjarib	A clan group of the Nyoongar people, the original inhabitants of the Pinjarra area in the south-west of Western Australia.
Biruk	One of the six Nyoongar seasons – when it is very hot in December and January.
boodjari	pregnant, mother-to-be

boomerang — Flat, curved wooden tool for hunting. Also used as a weapon and for digging. Also known as **kyalee**.

booyaiy — freshwater long-necked turtle

boya — Money – either pounds, shillings and pence, or dollars and cents.

Bunuru — One of the six Nyoongar seasons – when it is still hot but with the promise of cooler days in February and March.

dampa — Part of staple diet. Originally made with crushed grains from native plants, now made from dough – a mixture of flour and water, then cooked in ashes.

didjeridu — A musical instrument made from hollowed-out trees. For Nyoongars, only men are permitted to play it. Not a Nyoongar instrument. Introduced through trade, for hunting tools. Usually made from the mallee tree. Also known as yidaki.

dingo — Australian wild dog

Djeran — One of the six Nyoongar seasons – when the weather is cooler with signs of early rain in April and May.

Djilba — One of the six Nyoongar seasons – a time of new growth and flowers everywhere in August and September.

djoonah   big stick, usually made from heavy wood

djurripin   Happy for or about someone or something. Also
                jirripin: behave in a manner that shows you are
                romantically interested in someone, flirting with.

dwert   dog

goona   poop, shit, manure

goonamia   toilet, shit-house

gnoony   brother

gnummari   tobacco, cigarette

kaarda   big yellow-speckled goanna

kaarla   fire

kaartwarra   bad head, mentally challenged, crazy

kaep   water

Kambarang   One of the six Nyoongar seasons – when the
                days are warm and sunny around October and
                November.

karnyah   shame, feeling ashamed

kgaepa   alcohol – either wine, beer or spirits

koolungah   child, children

koomool	possum
koondee	very hard digging stick usually made from jarrah wood
koordah	brother
koort	heart
kwel	Australian native, member of the casuarina family
kyah	Can be a greeting or welcome. Also to say goodbye to someone who is leaving.
maaman	man, men
maarm bari	Small to medium-size tree found throughout Australia. Its seeds can be eaten once they have been roasted.
maarmbart	father, dad
Makuru	One of the six Nyoongar seasons – when the heavy showers come down in June and July.
mallee	Eucalyptus tree that grows with thick, knotted roots under the ground. Found throughout the country. Also used for making a didjeridu.
mardignu	sweetheart
mardong	to like someone

meeka	moon
mia-mia	house, home
milli-milli	paper
mimmi	breast
min-min	Unexplained small bright lights that appear out of nowhere. Can hover and travel in any direction.
moordgah	Christmas tree, a tree that has bright yellow or golden flowers that bloom at Christmas time.
moorditj	good, great, solid, strong, excellent
moorni	black
Moorni Kaep	Black Waters
Mulbpa	Clan group of Aboriginal people from the Pilbara area of Western Australia.
munartj	policeman
ninni	little, tiny
Nyoongar	Aboriginal people who live in the south-west corner of Western Australia from Geraldton to Esperance.

Palyku	Aboriginal people who are part of the Mulbpa clan group in the Pilbara. They come from the Nullagine and Marble Bar area of Western Australia.
Quinkan	An area in Queensland known for Aboriginal artwork and paintings in the Laura region.
unna	that's right, is that right?
waangkiny	talking, yarning with
wadjerlar	white person
waarlitj	wedge-tail eagle
waitj	emu
warra	bad, evil, not good
wiltja	similar to a gazebo, an open living area
winyarn	sad-looking, state of being poor, sorry-looking, submissive
Wongi	Clan group of Aboriginal people from the Kalgoorlie/Goldfields area of Western Australia.
Yamatji	Clan group of Aboriginal people from the Mid West of Western Australia.

Yawony	Name created by Nyoongar man Athol P. Hansen, using the first two letters of three of the major clan groups in Western Australia: Yamatji, Wongi and Nyoongar. It was the commercial arm of the original Ab-Trades business company.
yorga	woman, girl, female
yornah	blue-tongue goanna
yuntarn	black poisonous goanna, similar in size to kaarda

Scan here for an **online pronunciation guide**
to the words in Louise K. Hansen's Nyoongar
glossary, or go to our website:
fremantlepress.com.au.

ALSO AVAILABLE

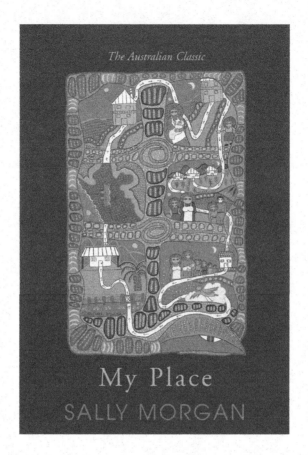

In 1982, Sally Morgan travelled back to her grandmother's birthplace. What started as a tentative search for information about her family turned into an overwhelming emotional and spiritual pilgrimage. *My Place* is a moving account of a search for truth into which a whole family is gradually drawn, finally freeing the tongues of the author's mother and grandmother, allowing them to tell their own stories.

'A book for everyone: a book with the form and texture of a novel and the complexity and pace of a mystery not solved until the final pages. It is wonderfully entertaining.' *New York Times Book Review*.

FROM FREMANTLEPRESS.COM.AU

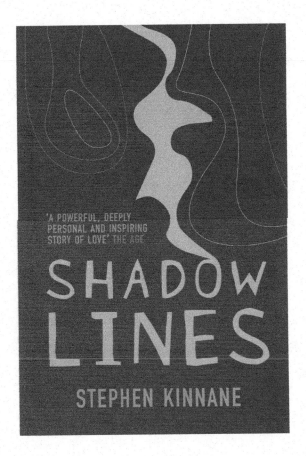

ALSO AVAILABLE

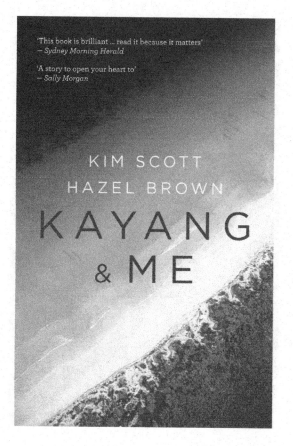

Award-winning novelist Kim Scott and Elder Hazel Brown have created a monumental family history of the Wilomin Noongar people. *Kayang and Me* is a powerful story of community and belonging, revealing the deep and enduring connections between family, country, culture and history that lie at the heart of Indigenous identity.

'... an exciting, vigorous and poignant history of an ancient people.' *West Australian*

'This book is brilliant. Read it because it is imaginatively conceived and beautifully crafted. And read it because it matters.' *Sydney Morning Herald*

FROM FREMANTLEPRESS.COM.AU

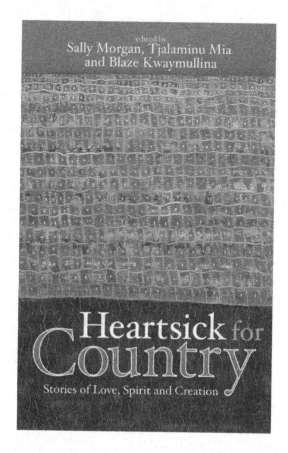

The stories in this anthology speak of the love between First Nations peoples and their countries. They are personal accounts that share knowledge, insight and emotion, each speaking of a deep connection to country and of feeling heartsick because of the harm that is being inflicted on country, through the logging of old growth forests, the conversion of millions of acres of land to salt fields, destruction of ancient rock art and significant sacred sites, and a record of species extinction that is the worst in the world.

'... voices that offer a way of seeing and relating to country which will allow the earth not only to survive, but to thrive.' *Ambelin Kwaymullina*

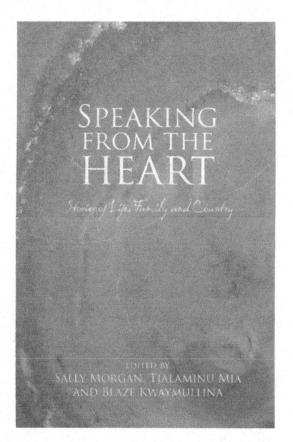

ALSO AVAILABLE

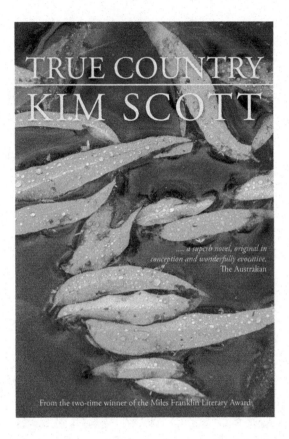

Billy, a young school teacher, arrives in Karnama, a remote settlement in Australia's far north, in search of his own history, his Aboriginality, and his future. Gradually the outsider is drawn in, and finds himself engaging deeply, irrevocably, not only with the moments of desolation and despair, but also with the great heart and spirit of the people. Finally the exile enters the true country.

'…captures the ambiguities, the troubles and the rewards which accompany the brutal and delicate nuances of relations when particles of one culture pass, as if through a fine sieve, into the heart of another culture.' *Elizabeth Jolley*

FROM FREMANTLEPRESS.COM.AU